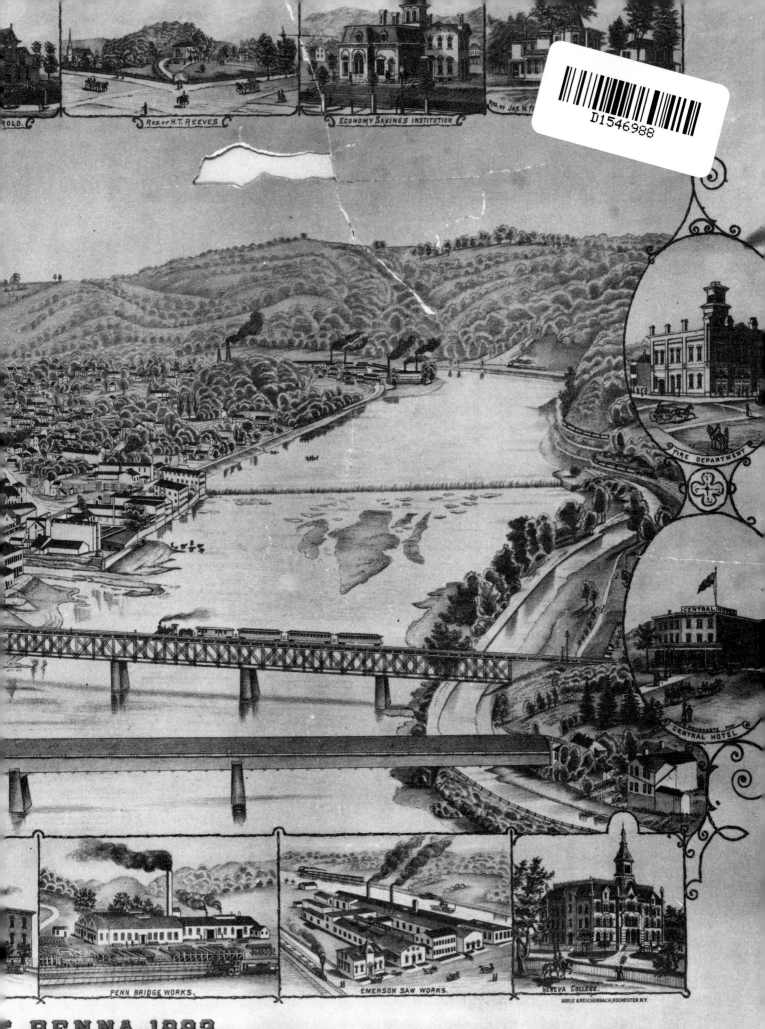

OLD.

RES. OF H.T. REEVES.

ECONOMY SAVINGS INSTITUTION

RES. OF JAS. M. F.

FIRE DEPARTMENT

CENTRAL HOTEL

PENN BRIDGE WORKS.

EMERSON SAW WORKS.

GENEVA COLLEGE.

KARLE & REICHENBACH, ROCHESTER, N.Y.

, PENNᴬ 1882.

Pro Christo et Patria
A History Of Geneva College

DAVID M. CARSON

THE ENTRANCE·OF·THY·WORD·GIVETH·LIGHT·

THE
BOOK
OF
BOOKS

Pro Christo et Patria
A History Of Geneva College

DAVID M. CARSON

THE
DONNING COMPANY
PUBLISHERS

To the Geneva family

without whom there would be no history to recount

Table of Contents

Pro Christo et Patria:

A History of Geneva College

Unless otherwise noted, photographs are from the Geneva College collections. Photographs credited to the Downie Collection have been lent by Rex Downie Jr., by Martha White Beard and Ruth White and by Theodora Downie Koble.

CIP/Copyright Data

Copyright © 1997 by Geneva College

All rights reserved, including the right to reproduce this work in any form whatsoever without permission in writing from the publisher, except for brief passages in connection with a review.

For information, write:
The Donning Company/Publishers
184 Business Park Drive, Suite 106
Virginia Beach, VA 23462

Steve Mull, General Manager
Debra Quesnel, Project Director
Tracey Emmons-Schneider, Director of Research
Dawn V. Kofroth, Assistant General Manager
Mary Jo Kurten, Editor
Joseph C. Schnellmann, Graphic Designer
Tony Lillis, Director of Marketing
Terri S. Arnold, Marketing Coordinator

Library of Congress Cataloging-in-Publication Data
Carson, David M., 1922–
       Pro Christo et patria : a history of Geneva College / by David M. Carson.
           p.   cm.
       Includes bibliographical references (p.) and index.
       ISBN 1-57864-006-7 (hardcover : alk. paper)
       1. Geneva College (Beaver Falls, Pa.)—History.   I.
Title. LD1891.G862C37   1997
  378.748'92—dc21   97-28094
                                     CIP

Printed in the United States of America

John Steuart Curry prepared this frontispiece for the 1920 *Genevan*, of which he was the art editor. Curry was later a well-known painter of the regionalist school, with paintings in many American museums. Among his best-known works are the murals in the Kansas State Capitol.

Foreword

For 150 years, Geneva College has been transforming minds, hearts, and lives for God's kingdom. Throughout those years, thousands of students experienced a higher education with a higher purpose.

This history is more than a chronology of events in the life of Geneva College. This history is the foundation of our careers and lives, nurtured by the Lord's people through the classrooms and residence halls of the campus. This history is the documentation of a vision of Christ-centered education which was formed around a cracker barrel.

Like a pebble thrown into a pond, so Geneva has created ever-widening ripples of change throughout the world. From Beaver Falls, Pennsylvania, to Apache Junction, Arizona, from Haiti to Egypt, from physicians and engineers to teachers and accountants, the college's alumni, employees, and friends have touched innumerable lives with the education and the Christian love they experienced at Geneva. All are ministers in the truest sense.

As an alumnus with a strong family history at Geneva, I convey my heartfelt appreciation to Dr. Carson for his gift that is this book. Our prayer is that as we read and remember, we may renew personal commitments to use our knowledge and gifts to continue God's work on earth. For this history is the story about changing lives through sharing the Geneva experience.

Ann O'Data Lawson, Class of 1987
President, Geneva Alumni Association

A recent picture of Old Main, the first building on the Beaver Falls campus of Geneva.

Acknowledgments

The people who have supported and assisted me in writing this history are legion, and to all of them I express my appreciation.

Special thanks go to President McFarland, who first suggested the project to me, and to President White, who persuaded me to undertake it and who has been a constant encourager. I want also to thank his assistant, Barbara McKenzie, for her cheerful answers to my many requests for information. I appreciate the confidence the Board of Trustees showed in opening the minutes of the board for my research.

Robin Ware, the coordinator of the sesquicentennial celebration, has made herself available to me whenever I needed advice and has taken many administrative responsibilities from my shoulders. Christina Townsend organized the illustrations for this volume.

The manuscript was read with great care by Galen Wilson and Lee Troup, and to them both I express my appreciation for their skillful editorial advice. It was also reviewed by four of my faculty colleagues, Professors S. S. Hanna, Paul Kilpatrick, Howard Mattsson-Boze, and Dean Smith, who faithfully combined suggestions with encouragement. Professor Hanna and Professor Harry Farra have done the laborious work of proofreading the manuscript.

My special thanks go also to Dr. Gerald Moran and his staff at McCartney Library. They provided hospitality for me during my research and writing, responded to my many requests for help, and encouraged me with their support. Marilyn VanDyke, the senior librarian in length of service, shared her knowledge of Geneva history. Vicki Mann used her archival skills in finding and organizing material.

The Office of Public Relations was very helpful. Mrs. Dee Hartman and her student assistant, Debbie Underhill, undertook picture searches far beyond the call of duty.

To the members of the Geneva community I express my gratitude for their interest in the history and for the specific ways in which they have helped and encouraged me.

This sign at the College Avenue entrance to Geneva identifies the college to the passerby.

Introduction

"Once upon a time . . . on April 20, 1848, to be exact."

When Geneva opened in 1848 (thirteen years before the great Civil War) in a tiny town in western Ohio, Geneva's founders could hardly have dreamed that their small school would have recognition as a leading Christian College.

Dr. David M. Carson, Samuel A. Sterrett Professor of Political Thought, Emeritus, has served Geneva with excellence for more than forty years, though he did not include his name when he mentioned a sampling of his contemporaries. He has crafted an insightful account of our century-and-a-half of service to God's Kingdom. This will enhance our understanding and appreciation of our godly heritage, and of many of the men and women who contributed sacrificially to Geneva's history.

The self-conscious effort in the 1960s to understand and reaffirm our historic roots as a Christian college climaxed in the adoption in 1967 of the *Foundational Concepts of Christian Education.* This renewed vision and commitment represent an unusual exception to the trend for institutions to deviate gradually from their Christian roots. In this sense, Geneva is blessed with a "youthful vitality" while enjoying the maturity of age. We are unashamed of our Christian roots and they are the very foundation of our contemporary relevance.

With the trustees, faculty, and administration, I am both humbled and challenged by the stewardship entrusted to us. We are grateful to the Lord for His faithfulness, and to our alumni, students, and friends, who share in giving Geneva its distinctive character. As we begin this 150th year, may we be encouraged and invigorated by God's grace to cooperate in building an even stronger college "*Pro Christo et Patria.*"

Dr. John H. White
President of Geneva College

President John Black Johnston
John Black Johnston (1802-1882) founded Geneva Hall and served as its president from 1848 to 1850. Johnston was the Reformed Presbyterian pastor in Northwood, a graduate of Franklin College in Ohio and of the Reformed Presbyterian Seminary. In 1848, he had just returned from an exploratory trip to the Caribbean that led him to recommend the establishment of a Reformed Presbyterian mission in Haiti.

ONE

A CURRICULUM OF STUDY

1848 — 1860

♠

────────────────

" *fter much deliberation*" *the presbytery agreed* "*to establish a Grammar School. The next morning Geneva Hall opened ... and as a college.*"

Carpe diem! Seize the day! It was April in Ohio. The year was 1848.The ministers and elders of the Reformed Presbyterian Presbytery of the Lakes were gathering in the small village of Northwood for their spring meeting. The fall before, John Black Johnston, the Northwood pastor, had proposed that the presbytery begin a "Grammar School," as a first step to eventually founding a college. Not wanting to act hastily, the members of the presbytery took the idea home to talk it over with their congregations. So now the proposal was on the agenda again. According to the official report of the meeting, "after much deliberation" the presbytery agreed "to establish a Grammar School."

Johnston seized the day. The *next morning* Geneva Hall opened for classes in its new brick building on the edge of Northwood, with a president (Johnston), a faculty (two young Milligan brothers), a curriculum, forty-two students . . . and as a college! The date was Thursday, April 20, 1848.

Johnston, familiar with the deliberate pace of deliberative bodies, and by temperament an activist, had acted before he had official approval. He had built a building and raised funds to pay for it—a

brick building that cost $1,454.30. He had recruited faculty and students. He had chosen a name, Geneva Hall, to set the college in the tradition of John Calvin and his city in Switzerland.

The earliest Ohio colleges were community enterprises, founded by people who wanted the opportunity of an education for their children. These colleges reflected the strongly Christian beliefs of their constituents, but they were not denominational. Toward the mid-century, however, denominations were realizing that if they were to retain the loyalty of their young people they would need to educate them in their own

Johnston purchased land on the edge of Northwood and built a brick building to house the college. The first classes were held in it April 20, 1848.

schools. Presbyterians, Baptists, Methodists, Lutherans, and Episcopalians founded colleges. Reflecting the thinking of the times, the Reformed Presbyterian Synod adopted in 1847 a report approving the establishment of a "literary institution" as "a highly desirable object," if practicable, and referring the matter to the presbyteries. Johnston decided that if a college was a desirable object, he would persuade the Presbytery of the Lakes that it was practicable.

When such colleges were founded, they were typically located in small towns, where morals were high and costs were low, far from the haunts of vice and the temptations of the city. Northwood, Johnston thought, provided an appropriate location for such a college—rural, but not inaccessible. Within two miles of Northwood ran the pioneer railroad of Ohio, called the Mad River and Lake Erie, brand new, connecting the village with Great Lakes steamers at Sandusky and with Ohio River boats at Cincinnati. In 1848 Northwood had suddenly become accessible to the whole denomination. There Johnston created a college—for Northwood and for the Reformed Presbyterian Church.

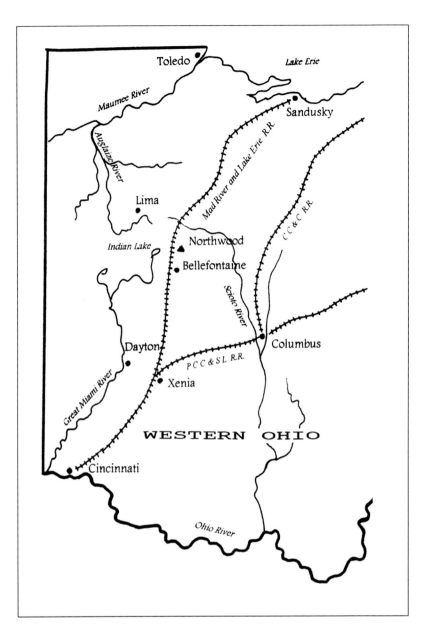

The village of Northwood was located in western Ohio, near the headwaters of the Miami River. By 1848 the Mad River and Lake Erie Railroad ran nearby.

GENEVA HALL.

This Christian College was founded by the Reformed Presbytery of the Lakes, April 1848, and located in Logan county, Ohio. The site is elevated, commanding an extensive view of the valley of the Miami, and of the surrounding beautiful and undulating country. The location is healthy, and in the neighborhood of medicinal sulphur springs; one of which is destined to be a place of resort for health and pleasure. It is within some 30 minute's walk of the Mad River and Lake Erie railroad, connecting Cincinnati on the Ohio river, and Sandusky city on Lake Erie;—and by the Lakes opening the shortest and cheapest route from New York City and the North Eastern States. The Columbus and Indianapolis rail road, which will connect with the Philadelphia and Pittsburg, and with the Baltimore and Ohio rail roads, will cross the former railroad at Bellefontaine, near "Geneva Hall," thus affording facilities for ready conveyance from every part of the Union.

The society surrounding is of an enterprising and industrious, and of a moral and religious character, embracing almost all the different denominations of evangelical christians.

As the institution is what it professes to be, Christian, and not Pagan, the Bible, with a selection from the best christian authors in the Learned Languages, will be the text book. The Latin course will embrace the following: Beza's Latin Testament, Grotius de Veritate, Buchanan's Psalms of David in Latin verse, Witsii Oeconomin, Calvini Institutio Religionis, and Institutio Theologiæ Elencticæ Francisco Turrettino. The Greek course—The Greek Testament, Chrysostom and Septuagint. The Hebrew—The Bible entire. The French—The Westminster Shorter Catechism, the New Testament, Psalms of David and a selection from the best christian French writers. Much of this extensive course, especially in the Latin and Hebrew is designed for students preparing for the christian ministry. It is designed that the whole course shall be thorough—raising, rather than lowering the standard of education. Students preparing for the ministry can well afford to take an enlarged course in the languages, such as are embraced in the class-books selected; all of which contain the very stamina of sound Theology. A graduate in this institution *may* be in advance of ordinary students of the second year, now in most of the Theological Seminaries in the United States. It is contemplated to prepare an entire system of moral science, based upon the Bible —The Moral Law being the rule of moral duties, and the foundation of all moral science, and should be our text-book. The best selection of text-books in the Mathematical course, and in the Natural, Mental and Moral sciences will be made, having regard to the christian character of the Institution. Students of almost any denomination can have access to their respective churches within ordinary church-going distance. None will be compelled to attend places of worship not of their own faith; but all will be required to observe the Sabbath, and preserve a strict moral decorum.

As a female department will be connected with the Institution, it will be conducted by a separate teacher; and recitations will be heard in a separate apartment.—All the branches usually taught in the best Female Seminaries, will be taught in this Institution by a finished and extensive scholar—a graduate of the Western University of Pennsylvania.

Boarding can be had as cheap as in any other part of the United States—being *in Ohio*, in the great *Miami valley*, teeming with luxuries and staple provisions surpassed, perhaps, by no other portion of the globe. The medium and usual price $1 per week—lower to those who take rooms which will be given gratis in the College buildings. Tuition in College $8 per session, or half year—in the preparatory school less. Summer session will open last Monday of April.

FACULTY.

Rev. J. B. JOHNSTON, Principal,

JOHN KNOX MILLIGAN, Professor of Languages and Mathematics,

JAMES SAURIN MILLIGAN, Tutor and Assistant in Prep. School.

Pecuniary aid from the patrons and friends of literature is respectfully solicited.

March 3, 1849.

This early circular, reprinted in *The Geneva Book*, is the oldest surviving Geneva catalog. It describes the first curriculum and urges the attractions of the Northwood community.

A later view of Northwood's main street, which lost some of its activity when the college moved to Beaver Falls.

W. M. Glasgow drew this map of his hometown of Northwood for his 1908 history, *The Geneva Book*.

Students then, as now, took out some of their frustrations through journalism. The earliest surviving example of unauthorized publication was entitled, with a sidelong glance at the more famous Westminster Assembly document, "The Northwood Catechism." The opening questions have some fun with the official college publicity:

The Northwood Catechism 1850
Ridentem discere verum quid vetat. . .
[Roughly translated: through laughter to learn the forbidden truth]

Q. Where is Northwood?
A: In the Great Miami Valley.
Q: How is it situated?
A: High, commanding an extensive view.
Q: Of what?
A: Of frog ponds.
Q: How far can you see?
A: Beyond the sun and moon, even to the North Star.
Q: But, how far can you see around?
A: 'Tis an immense distance, perhaps a quarter of a mile.
Q: By what kind of country is it surrounded?
A: One "beautiful and undulating."
Q: What undulations are visible?
A: Those of swamps and stagnant ponds.
[and so it continues]

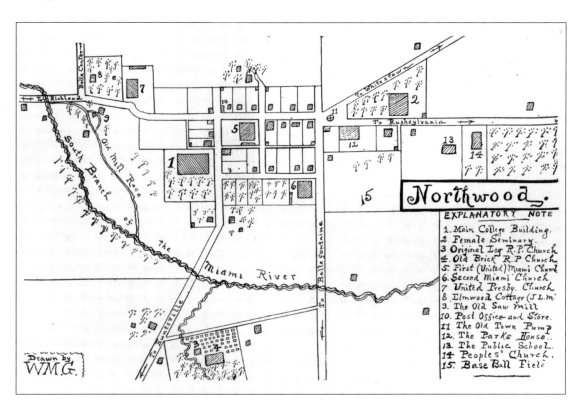

President William Finney George
William Finney George (1821–1880), like Johnston, was an alumnus of Franklin College, Ohio. When the elected president declined the office, George served as interim president from 1850 to 1852. In 1852, he resigned to accept a pastorate in Macedon, Ohio, serving later in Coulterville and Staunton, Illinois.

In the middle of the nineteenth century, what did it mean to be an educated person? It was assumed that central to Western culture was a body of knowledge, based on the Latin and Greek classics and transmitted across the Christian centuries through European universities. To be educated was to be acquainted with that body of knowledge, which was not part of the daily experience of most Americans, and which therefore set one apart. It was also assumed that through the attention to detail necessary to learn the classical languages, one's mental faculties would be sharpened. It was not assumed that this experience would train one for the professions—that would come in seminary, in medical school, or by reading law. But before one could do that, one must "get an education."

Geneva Hall began with a challenge to that view, short-lived, but important in understanding the roots of the college. Johnston had been influenced in his thinking about college education by the writings of an older Reformed Presbyterian minister, James Renwick Willson. Willson opposed the tradition; he believed strongly that reading the "pagan classics" was not preparation for a faithful Christian life. In an 1848 article he wrote:

The vices of the heathen world are garnished in our collegiate class books, with all the adornments of poetic and other beauties of style. With these, the youthful mind is fascinated. A taste for paganized poetry . . . is acquired, and it must be gratified at the expense of everlasting perdition.

To avoid such an outcome, the first Geneva students therefore learned their Latin, not from Caesar, Cicero, and Virgil, but from Calvin's *Institutes*, Buchanan's translation of the *Psalms*, and from other authors of the Reformation period. They learned Greek,

not from Plato, Homer, and Sophocles, but from the Greek New Testament, the Septuagint, and Chrysostom.

That curriculum, however, was so much at odds with the culture of the time that it did not long outlive Johnston's brief presidency. When J. R. W. Sloane was chosen the third president in 1852, he made it clear in his inaugural address that he did not intend to maintain it, though he did intend that the college be distinctively Christian, possessing "a curriculum of study from no part of which the Bible has been excluded."

Everyone took the same "curriculum of study," whether it was Johnston's or Sloane's. All Geneva students sat in the same classes, had the same professors, and studied the same material. When they graduated they would "have an education"; they could then proceed to train for their chosen vocations and would help create an atmosphere of culture in their homes and communities.

Given the nature of the curriculum, the process of "getting an education" centered around recitation, testing whether students had mastered that portion of the body of knowledge assigned for the day. Students came to class, sat on benches, were called on one after another to recite. In a class of Greek or Latin, they would be asked to "parse" any part of the text assigned—that is, to explain the grammatical form of each word, its meaning and usage, and to translate the passage precisely. In mathematics they would present their solutions to the assigned problems. In the few courses where there was a textbook, they would be prepared to "recite" the assigned pages. Thus professors were said to "hear classes."

Such a procedure would seem to offer little opportunity for "teaching" in the modern understanding of the term. Indeed, once a person had been through such a course, he was immediately prepared to hear other students recite it. This meant that the early teachers at Geneva were young men. John Calvin Knox Milligan was named Professor of Languages and Mathematics when he was nineteen. Even through the recitation process, however, a good teacher would communicate, and it is clear from many comments that the quality and breadth of instruction left their mark on Geneva students. It is also true that the ideal student in such a curriculum need not be creative or a critical thinker. In the 1850s President Sloane praised the students he taught as being "diligent, orderly, and moral." President George in the 1870s stated as his purpose to bring students to "the highest level of accuracy and thoroughness." For such goals the recitation was a defensible procedure.

One escape from such a regimen was through the literary society, a nearly universal part of American college life in those years. In the society students came into contact with the contemporary world and their creative and critical skills were challenged and developed. About 1853,

Geneva's two original societies were combined into the Union Lit, which played a major role in the life of Geneva men. Its importance in the college culture was symbolized by the room where it met, a room reserved for the society and elaborately furnished by society members. At a time when annual tuition was $16, one student contributed $20 for furnishing the room; in total the members raised $100 (at a time when the president's salary was $300). The society created an island of elegance in an otherwise spartan building, with papered walls and venetian blinds—and a treasured carpet. The rule was that members had to leave their muddy boots at the door and don prescribed Moroccan leather slippers. Programs at the weekly meetings featured original essays and orations, dramatic and humorous readings, with a debate to climax the evening. Debates were serious and on varied questions:

Is it probable that the earth has existed for a longer period than 6000 years?

Is the love of liquor a stronger passion than the love of women?

President James Renwick Willson Sloane
James Renwick Willson Sloane (1823-1886), a graduate of Jefferson College, was the president of Geneva from 1852 to 1856. He resigned from the presidency to serve as pastor of the Third Reformed Presbyterian Church of New York City and was later a professor in the Reformed Presbyterian Seminary. From 1878 to 1886 he served as president of the Geneva Board of Trustees. His wife, Margaret Milligan Sloane, was the capable headmistress of the Female Seminary until her death in 1854.

Hazing

[The rural location of Northwood provided other forms of education for the unwary.]

In its multiplied forms hazing was practiced through the whole history of the College at Northwood. The masked cohort with the hangman's rope; the shooting from ambush or by decoy into some sequestered place; the "going sniping" into the meshes of some vast forest at midnight—all had the one end in view, viz.: the initiation of the precocious or verdant metropolitan youth into the common ways of the rural community. . . .

Sometimes the verdant youths were captured, taken into a large pasture field and tied to the backs of a few bucking colts upon which never man sat. In order to encourage the equally uninitiated equines to do their best upon such occasions, they were spurred and frightened to the point of madness. It was agreed that these victims put to shame any Wild West performance, or made tame the celebrated ride of Paul Revere, as they chased and counter-raced the six acre pasture field. . . .

W. M. Glasgow, *The Geneva Book*, 1908

Is it the duty of all Christian nations to establish arbitration in their treaties as the mode, and the only mode, of settling international disputes?

Especially, in this decade before the Civil War, the debates were about slavery:

Resolved: That the different features and complexions of the human race are the effects of climate, education, and habits of life.

Resolved: That the United States Constitution sanctions slavery.

Resolved: That the principles and policies of the Whig Party are better calculated to abolish slavery than those of the Freesoilers. (Then, as now, should reformers best work within the party system or through a third party?)

Given the nature of the subject matter and the sentiment of the community, the society agreed that after each debate there should be two votes, which side did the better debating, and which side was morally in the right!

Both college and community were strongly abolitionist. When the Fugitive Slave Act was passed in 1850, requiring that slaves who managed to escape be returned to their masters, and forbidding anyone to aid their escape or hinder their recapture, a meeting was called in Northwood "for considering the duty of Christians." Addressed by faculty members, the meeting passed resolutions describing the law as "impolitic, inhuman, oppressive, and God-dishonoring," and promising to "still feed the hungry, clothe the naked, and hide the outcasts, whether white or black, doing to others as we would have them do to us." Northwood was strategically located on the Underground Railroad between the Ohio River and Lake Erie, and faculty and students kept their word.

President John Calvin Knox Milligan
John Calvin Knox Milligan (1829–1906) was one of the original faculty members at Geneva Hall and served as president from 1856 to 1858. He resigned to become pastor of the First Reformed Presbyterian Church of New York City. He married Rachel Farrington, a teacher in the Female Seminary.

President John Calvin Smith
John Calvin Smith (1831–1900) served as president from 1858 to 1860. When support for the college faded away, he entered the Reformed Presbyterian Seminary and later served pastorates near New Castle, Pennsylvania, and in Cincinnati.

[Thirteen fugitives were taken from the Quaker settlement] by various roads into Northwood and distributed to different stations, including the cave [on Isaac Patterson's farm] to spend a fortnight. Then they were all shifted, and a week later taken by ten [Geneva Hall] students, disguised and armed as hunters, in two covered wagons on the road for Sandusky, some ninety miles distant. Professor J. S. T. Milligan, of the college faculty, went by train . . . [to Sandusky] to engage passage for the Negroes on the *Bay City* steamboat across the lake to Fort Malden. . . . The "hunters," some of them of big frame and all of them able bodies and resolute, told Mr. Milligan their experience, which was often thrilling and sometimes amusing. Interest was frequently shown on the part of the spectators to get a satisfactory look at the "thirteen deer" brought out of the woods. . . . However, they always respected the firm command to "stand back." . . . Forced marches by night and by day soon enabled the occupants of the wagons to embark on the steamboat . . . and land in due time on Canadian soil.

W. H. Siebert, *The Mysteries of Ohio's Underground Railroads*, Columbus, Ohio, 1951, 151–152.

Along with educating its sons, the Northwood community was concerned about the education of women. Three years after Geneva Hall opened, Johnston and his wife, Elizabeth Boyd Johnston, established a Female Seminary, "seeking the patronage of friends who have daughters to educate." For the purpose they built a large building at the other end of Northwood's short main street. In the original prospectus Johnston announced that "the scholars will have access to lectures in the College and to the college apparatus and the Library." Some teachers taught in both schools. Students had opportunity, for a fee, to have lessons in music and drawing, arts appropriate for the refined woman. But it

seems clear that the purpose of the Seminary was to provide an education for women comparable to that of men. The Seminary students had their own literary society, the Partheno-Kosmean (The Maidens' World), which met weekly. For their annual meeting one year, they invited as their guest a local judge who spoke on the topic "The Claims of Female Education Founded on the Duties and Responsibilities of American Women," and they printed his address for circulation. (That the women had their own society, let it be noted, did not prevent numerous occasions when the "Seminoles," i.e. the Seminary women, were invited to Union Lit meetings.)

An 1856 prospectus for the Female Seminary emphasizes the quality of its faculty.

In the beginning, Geneva's budget seemed simple. When Johnston built and furnished the original building for Geneva Hall, he secured subscriptions from the community and the denomination to pay for all but $66.81 of the cost, which he then contributed to the cause. So much for capital costs. Faculty salaries were paid by offering the president three-sevenths of what tuition income there was; each of the other two faculty members received two-sevenths. Utility bills were met by charging students twenty-five cents each winter term for wood. Such a budget seems automatically balanced.

However, even from the beginning, debts began to appear—acquiring some "philosophical apparatus" (i.e. equipment for demonstrating scientific experiments); an account at the local store; debts to individuals for unspecified purposes. The board found it difficult to get contributions to pay off such unbudgeted items. Ironically, it was Geneva's success that turned these difficulties into a crisis. When Geneva Hall

This building, built at the other end of Northwood's main street in 1851, housed the Female Seminary. After Geneva became coeducational, it served as a dormitory for women until the college moved to Beaver Falls.

opened, it met in the small building Johnston had erected for it: twenty-five by forty feet, with two stories. As enrollment grew under the able leadership of President Sloane, the board borrowed money to enlarge and remodel the original building, more than doubling its dimensions and adding a third story. The college was not able either to amortize the debt thus incurred, or in fact to keep the annual budget current. Neither from the neighborhood nor from the denomination was there adequate financial support. Sloane resigned, discouraged, and grieving over the death of his wife.

In 1857, the Presbytery of the Lakes gladly offered its official responsibility for Geneva Hall to the Synod of the denomination. At its 1859 meeting the Synod reluctantly accepted the gift, but left the existing board to flounder, offering advice but no money. The last minutes of the board, dated July 7, 1859, ended with an appeal for financial support that did not come. The college faded away. The Female Seminary closed. Students went to fight in the Civil War. Teachers went to other occupations. All that remained in Northwood were the buildings and the memories.

As the college enrollment grew, the trustees enlarged the original building in 1853, doubling its dimensions and adding a third story.

President Nathan Robinson Johnston
Nathan Robinson Johnston (1820–1904) was invited to reopen Geneva after the Civil War. He acted as president from 1865 to 1867. His autobiography, *Looking Back from the Sunset Land*, recounts his varied life, including fifteen years as missionary to Chinese immigrants in Oakland, California. His wife, Rosamond Rogers Johnston, taught with him at Geneva.

TWO

Geneva Hall Becomes Geneva College
1860—1880

*P*resident George created from the mere shadow of a college a stable and effective institution.

As the Civil War neared its end, the buildings and the memories of Geneva were still in Northwood. There were people in the community who very much wanted to have a college again, and specifically a college that would be Reformed Presbyterian. Five of them, including Johnston's brother and sister and John L. McCartney, a Reformed Presbyterian pastor, gained ownership of the college building. In October 1864, they asked Nathan R. Johnston, another brother of the founder and the pastor of the Reformed Presbyterian congregation in Topsham, Vermont, to reopen the college, apparently as a private venture to be supported by tuition. Johnston and his wife came, and classes began in January 1865, with sixteen students, and as a coeducational institution. At the same time, Reformed Presbyterians had been without a college long enough to realize the utility of a denominational college in preparing students to enter the seminary and the ministry of the church. With that in mind, the Synod of 1865 appointed a board of education to "take measures for establishing a school," pre-

President Samuel John Crowe
Samuel John Crowe (1843–1931) was a graduate of Westminster College. He was president for four years at a very discouraging time in Geneva's history, from 1867 to 1871. After his presidency he served several Reformed Presbyterian pastorates. His wife, Amanda Geddes Crowe, taught science and instrumental music while her husband was president.

sumably at Northwood. The relationship of these two attempts to reopen the college is hard to unravel after the passage of years; but it was not without friction.

That confused relationship was further complicated by a third motivation for reopening Geneva, a remarkable proposal by Rev. John McCartney, one of the owners of the college building. McCartney was deeply moved by the plight of the freedmen in the South, no longer slaves, but without education, without leadership, and often without the gospel. The Reformed Presbyterian Church had during the war carried on extensive mission work among the freedmen in the South; a number of Geneva students from the 1850s were working there. The church was therefore aware of the need and increasingly aware that more effective service could be provided by training freedmen themselves to work in the South. McCartney proposed that the college at Northwood be reopened to provide education for a selected group of freedmen who would return to the South as ministers of the

Left: Daniel Boxley was one of the students attracted to Geneva by its program for freedmen. After earning the A.B. degree in 1873, he taught for several years in Knox Academy, at Selma, Alabama, and in Rolla, Missouri. Later he worked as a mail carrier and hotel clerk. By 1908 he was a rancher in Franklin County, Washington.

Right: John L. McCartney, a Reformed Presbyterian pastor in Northwood, was influential in reopening Geneva after the Civil War. It was his great desire to educate freedmen. He taught science in Geneva both at Northwood and at Beaver Falls.

FREEDMEN'S COLLEGE,
Northwood, Logan Co., Ohio,

_____ *186* .

DEAR SIR :

    The Synod of the REFORMED PRESBYTERIAN CHURCH has established an institution for the thorough education of colored Boys and Girls from among the Freedmen of the South. Believing that the colored race need most of all educated men, of their own color, as teachers, preachers, physicians and advocates, we propose to give, to at least a limited number, a complete *Academical* training. The entire system of instruction will be conducted with a view to their becoming missionaries among their own people. We have ample facilities for the work we propose. The Board, if necessary, will be at the whole expense of boarding, clothing and tuition. In view of this only those of superior natural talents will be accepted. We propose operating especially with two classes—

    1st. Boys and Girls of superior mind and fair promise, from twelve to twenty-one years of age, whom we should desire to retain for a number of years in the institution.

    2d. Talented young preachers and teachers among the colored people, who with one year's training in our school, might be greatly aided in their work.

    We desire the aid of all teachers among the Freedmen in securing for the institution pupils of the right sort. Can you recommend to us a suitable boy or girl? If so, will you answer immediately, as far as you can, the following queries :

    1. How old? 2. Color? 3. Features? 4. Family connections? 5. Peculiarity of his talents and disposition? 6. Moral character? 7. His history as far as known? 8. His purpose in securing an education? 9. Could he bear part of his own expenses? 10. Can you raise means sufficient to forward him to us?

    Please answer at once, and give any other information you may think desirable.

        Address,

            J. L. McCARTNEY,

                Secretary of the Board,

                 BELLE CENTRE, O.

McCartney distributed a prospectus as a means of contacting freedmen who might enroll at Geneva. He promised them a "complete *Academical* training."

gospel and as teachers. Synod agreed enthusiastically. McCartney corresponded with representatives of the U.S. Freedmen's Bureau; he contacted Reformed Presbyterian missionaries in the South; he sent a circular to others who might know of suitable candidates. There was a good response, both of possible beneficiaries and of money from the denomination to provide for their support. As a result, well into the 1880s there were African-Americans from the South in the student body. This social concern, opening a college in the North to freedmen, was uncommon in the post-Civil War period. The church was rewarded for its concern and its financial support by black graduates, Lewis Johnston, G. M. Elliott, and later Solomon Kingston, who served as pastors of the African-American Reformed Presbyterian congregation in Selma, Alabama, and others who taught in Knox Academy, a school established in Selma by the denomination. In broader terms, the education of freedmen did not have the effect for which McCartney hoped: few of the students returned to the South, and those who remained in the North found opportunities very restricted.

Despite these combined motivations for reopening Geneva, the college encountered difficulties. Financial planning proved unrealistic. Income from tuition did not cover costs, especially when children of ministers and the students from the South were "beneficiaries," entitled to free tuition. There had to be financial support beyond tuition. Therefore, each year Synod announced a goal for contributions to Geneva, typically $1,500 or $2,000, enough to keep the college solvent. To raise this sum, congregations were directed to take a collection for the college at one Sabbath service during the year. But congregations did not always respond; and when they did, the typical offering was disappointingly minimal. Usually about one-third of Synod's goal was raised; this went largely to pay tuition and support for the "beneficiaries," and was not a contribution beyond tuition. Each year the treasurer reported a "balanced" budget to Synod, but each year noted the growing sum owed to faculty members!

Discouragement took root among both board and faculty. In the summer of 1870 the entire faculty resigned to pursue theological studies, and the board submitted its collective resignation to Synod. Synod's response did not suggest much of a future for Geneva. It appointed a new board of four members, all from the Presbytery of the Lakes, suggesting that the denomination was washing its hands of the college and returning it to local control. Its proposal for the college was that the two Reformed Presbyterian ministers in Northwood, John L. McCartney and William Milroy, both of whom had been hearing classes, be responsible for the college. The shades of night seemed to be falling again.

Geneva might have sunk into oblivion but for the fact that one of the members of the new board was Henry Hosick George, pastor of the Reformed Presbyterian congregation in Cincinnati.

For half a century Geneva graduates, both white and African-American, taught in Knox Academy in Selma, Alabama. It was founded by Reformed Presbyterians in 1874 to provide education largely denied to African-Americans in the South. This is a picture of the Knox Academy Band.

President Henry Hosick George
Henry Hosick George (1833–1914) was elected president in 1872 and served until 1890, far longer than any president before him. He was the first Geneva alumnus to serve as president. He revived the college at a critical time in its history and later presided over its move to Beaver Falls, Pennsylvania, in 1880.

For two years, he managed by various devices and with the help of McCartney and Milroy to keep the college alive. In 1872, Synod elected him as president. During the eighteen years of his presidency, he created from the mere shadow of a college a stable and effective institution. Earlier presidents had seen themselves as teachers first of all—it was their job to teach, and to teach well, the students who came—and to try to subsist on the tuition the students provided. George not only taught, and taught well, but also saw the life and prosperity of the college as his responsibility. In his two years as chairman of the board before becoming president, he developed a clear sense of mission for the college and

FACULTY.

Rev. H. H. GEORGE,
President and Professor of Greek and Moral Science.

Rev. WILLIAM MILROY,
Professor of Latin and Mental Science.

Rev. J. L. McCARTNEY,
Professor of Mathematics, Natural Philosophy, and Astronomy.

N. R. JOHNSTON, A. M.,
Professor of Natural Science, and Adjunct Professor of Language.

ROSAMOND R. JOHNSTON,
English and Normal Department, and Adjunct Professor of Mathematics.

INSTRUMENTAL MUSIC.

BOARD OF TRUSTEES.

COURSE OF STUDY.

PREPARATORY DEPARTMENT.

FIRST YEAR.

First Term.	Second Term.	Third Term.
Arithmetic. English Grammar. Latin Lessons.	Arithmetic, Higher. Geography. Elementary Algebra. English Composition. Latin Grammar and Reader.	Elementary Algebra. History. Higher Arithmetic. English Composition. Cæsar.

SECOND YEAR.

First Term.	Second Term.	Third Term.
Algebra. Cæsar finished and Virgil begun. Greek Lessons. English Composition.	Algebra. English Composition. Virgil finished. Greek Reader.	Algebra. English Composition. Cicero's Orations. Anabasis.

COLLEGIATE DEPARTMENT.

FRESHMAN YEAR.

First Term.	Second Term.	Third Term.
Algebra Reviewed. Geometry. Sallust and Latin Composition. Herodotus.	Geometry Continued. Horace's Odes and Epistles. Memorabilia.	Geometry Completed. Livy and Latin Composition. Homer's Iliad.

SOPHOMORE YEAR.

First Term.	Second Term.	Third Term.
Plain Trigonometry. Cicero de Senectute. Homer's Odyssey.	Analytical Geometry and Surveying. Juvenal. Demosthenes de Corona.	Spherical Trigonometry. Horace, Satires and Epistles. Euripides.

how it could move toward accomplishing that mission. At once things began to happen. He promoted the college energetically, lecturing on educational matters to publicize the college, writing personal letters to potential students, and distributing thousands of circulars.

The college took on new vigor. The president resurrected the 1855 charter; Geneva Hall became Geneva College; degrees were again granted. The village of Northwood, caught up by his enthusiasm, changed its name to West Geneva and contributed funds to renovate the college building. To encourage growth, George broadened the appeal of the college program. For example, the college began granting the bachelor of science degree. Despite the title, it was in fact a three-year course, instead of the usual four years, offering no more science than in the B.A. program, shortening the time by omitting Greek and some mathematics and adding two years of German. Students who had no professional use for four years of Greek found it attractive. The president also experimented briefly with a commercial department, offering courses in bookkeeping, banking, railroading, and steamboating! Attendance rose dramatically, from about 50 students before George became president to 170 two years later. Synod responded by enlarging the board to include members representing each presbytery to broaden

Below: A copy of the first catalog of George's presidency survives. It lists the curriculum for both the two preparatory and the four college years. Registration was simple: all students took the same courses. (Though their names were listed in the catalog, the Johnstons resigned to become missionaries in Minnesota.)

JUNIOR YEAR.

First Term.	Second Term.	Third Term.
Calculus.	Nat. Philosophy Completed.	Geology.
Natural Philosophy.	Astronomy.	Mechanical.
Horace Ars Poetica.	Sophocles.	Political Economy.
		Greek Testament.

SENIOR YEAR.

First Term.	Second Term.	Third Term.
Chemistry.	Chemistry Continued.	Zoology.
Rhetoric.	Logic.	Evidences of Christianity.
Mental Philosophy.	Moral Philosophy.	Physical Geography.
Greek Testament and Hebrew.	Constitutional Law.	Greek Testament and Hebrew.
	Greek Testament and Hebrew.	

REMARK.—It will appear from the above course, particularly in the Preparatory Department, that special attention will be given to the English branches, as we are assured that the mastery of these lies fundamental to all solid and substantial education.

TUITION.

Classical Department, per term...$10 00
Normal and Scientific Department, per term 8 00
Where three students are sent from one family in the latter
    Department 20 00
All tuition paid in advance.

BOARDING.

Ample provisions will be made for young ladies in the seminary building, which will be under the control of President George, and no effort will be spared to make it a quiet and comfortable home for such. Boarding there will not exceed $3 00, exclusive of incidentals, such as light, fuel, etc., and $3 50 including these.

As it is the aim to put the price as low as good boarding can be furnished for, the pupils will be expected to bring their own towels and toilet articles, sheets and pillow-slips, and a blanket each.

There are boarding places in the village where young gentlemen can be accommodated at very reasonable rates. If economy is desired, rooms can be had at $1.00 per month, and by clubbing together, furnishing their own provisions, and procuring a lady to cook, their boarding need not exceed $2.00 per week; it may fall even below that, but they can board well at $2.00 each. Every effort will be made to afford facilities to students for thus clubbing together.

SITUATION OF GENEVA COLLEGE.

It is located at Northwood, Logan county, Ohio, near Belle Center, on the Cincinnati & Sandusky Railroad. It is easy of access by two leading railways, and by a new and excellent turnpike road leading through Belle Center and Northwood to Bellefontaine. In an elevated and healthful position; in a community eminent for intelligence and evangelical religion; and in a village wholly free from the ordinary temptations to vice and immorality to which students at college are generally exposed, the Institution is most desirably located.

AIMS OF THE INSTITUTION.

1st. Thoroughness of scholarship; in all important branches of education to know no superior. With a newly organized faculty we resolve anew to make complete scholars.

2d. To make all instructions of the most practical kind, by lectures, demonstrations, and experiments; mastering each subject of investigation, so that the student may be fitted for any of the active duties of life to which he may turn his attention.

3d. To guard carefully the students' moral and religious character, exercising a kind and parental authority, impressing self-respect, urging to worthy motives and noble efforts, and discountenancing immorality of whatever kind it may be.

TO THE FRIENDS OF EDUCATION.

We ask you to give us your patronage. Under the blessing of a kind Providence we hope to succeed. We shall spare no pains to make ours an Institution of the first grade. If you intrust to us your sons and your daughters we shall not slacken our efforts to give you entire satisfaction. And we firmly believe that a trial will secure your subsequent patronage.

All letters desiring a circular catalogue or fuller information should be addressed to the President, Rev. H. H. GEORGE, 109 Clinton street, Cincinnati, O., until the first of August; after that his address will be Belle Center, Logan county, O.

The next Term will begin Tuesday, September 10, 1872. It is very desirable that all students should be present on the first day.

The stone marks the site of the college building in Northwood. It was erected by the Logan County Historical Society in 1948 on the occasion of Geneva's centennial.

GENEVA COLLEGE
ESTABLISHED HERE IN 1848
BY DR. J. B. JOHNSTON
MOVED TO BEAVER FALLS PA. IN 1879
ERECTED BY
LOGAN CO. HISTORICAL SOCIETY

the base of support. Articles appeared in the church magazine urging the patronage of the denomination. As W. Melancthon Glasgow remarked in his *The Geneva Book*, "The 'quivering age' should terminate with 1872."

During the 1870s, the history of Geneva's literary societies entered a new phase. In 1870 the Aletheorian Society (named from the Greek word for *truth*) was reorganized; and in 1872 it was joined by the Adelphic Society (from the Greek word for *brother*, because the Aletheorians briefly excluded the freedmen from their society). From the beginning, both societies were coeducational. For half a century these two

Course of Study.

First Academic Year.
First Term—Brown's Short and Easy Questions for Children.
Second Term—McCartney's Scotch Primer for Babies.
Third Term—Lind's Irish Literature.

Second Academic Year.
First Term—Elementary Composition.
Second Term—The Shorter Catechism.
Third Term—George's Chapel Orations.

Freshman Year.
First Term—The larger Catechism.
Second Term—The Book of Psalms.
Third Term—The Confession of Faith and the R. P. Testimony.

Sophomore Year.
First Term—Surveying Turnip Patches.
Second Term—Comic Sections.
Third Term—Scientific Chicken Stealing.

Junior Year.
First Term—Taking Physics after Fizzles.
Second Term—Making Remarks at Prayermeetings.
Third Term—Asking the Blessing and Returning Thanks.

Senior Year.
First Term—Milroy's Art of Courting, George's Comparative Philology, Seminary Lectures at 1-o'clock A. M., and Debates on Buggy Stealing.
Second Term—Debates on Destructiveness to Fowls, Art of Pleasing Young Ladies, and Elementary Prayers at Prayer Meetings.
Third Term—The Art of Having Worship, Christian Experience, Belles Letters, and Packing for the Seminary.
  The Sophomore, Junior and Senior Classes all attend Vincent's Theater, and are drilled in chewing tobacco, and smoking cigars, during the winter term. The four classes in the Collegiate departments will take systematic buggy-rides.
  Normal and Scientific Course subject to *perpetual change*.

Calendar for 1879-80.

First Term beginning Wednesday, September 3rd, ends Tuesday, November 25th, provided the Faculty are all present.
  Professors vacations monthly, of one week each.
  Hollow eve, October 31st.
  Display of *rose buds* and others Tuesday eve., November 25th.
  Second Term begins Wednesday, November 26th, at which time the students will assemble for Thanksgiving.
  Students vacation 8 days, and Faculty vacation 28 days, commencing on Wednesday, December 24th.
  Day of Prayer for College Faculties, Saturday, January 24th, 1880.
  Celebration of St. Valentine's day, February 14th; Henry's birthday, February 22nd.
  Third term begins Wednesday, February 25th.
  Junior Entertainment, Friday, April 3rd.
  Contest between Faculty and students, Friday, April 17th.
  Reunion of Faculty and their families, May 3rd.
  Examinations of Sophomores guilty of not living up to the requirements of the course laid down in the catalogue, Friday and Monday, May 15th and 18th.
  Baccalaureate sermon by Joe Wylie, Sabbath May 17th.
  Pelting sheep day, Monday, May 15th.
  Chicken eaters reunion, Tuesday, May 17th.
  Day for distributing sheepskins, May 20th. Afterward, falling of houses, crushing of timbers, consummation of all things.
  For further information address
          HON. HENRY GEORGE, D. D.,
                    Northwood, Ohio.

These satirical excerpts are an example of student journalism of the time. This "catalog" was published during Geneva's last year at Northwood and reflects student resentment over the decision to move the college to Beaver Falls.

societies—with their rivalry for members, their weekly meetings, and their annual contests—dominated the social life of the college and developed the forensic talents of generations of Geneva students. The topics for the debates in the 1870s were not always so serious as those of the Union Lit in the 1850s: "Resolved: That it is easier to ride a horse to water than to water him down in the well," or "Resolved: That woman has the inalienable right to the ascendancy half the time." But for the annual contests, the societies debated questions of national and international import, among them whether it was appropriate to educate women, and (on the occasion of the revolution that overthrew Napoleon III) whether a republican government would survive in France. These annual contests were occasions of great rivalry, so intense in fact that the faculty ended the competitions in 1878, and they were not revived for nearly a decade.

Team sports at Geneva began after the Civil War, as the returning veterans brought the game of baseball from army camps to towns across the country—including Northwood. The first baseball team at Geneva was organized in 1868; the captain of the team and its pitcher was the then president of the college, S. J. Crowe. During the later 1870s a regular team was maintained, playing the teams from neighboring towns. The final year at Northwood the team was undefeated, with the future college historian, "Lank" Glasgow, as its storied pitcher.

Mattie Wylie, Class of 1875, was one of the first Geneva graduates to serve as a foreign missionary. This excerpt is part of a letter she wrote from Latakia, Syria, in 1878, to Mrs. J. C. Boyd, a pastor's wife in Utica, Ohio, thanking her for a gift of clothing for the girls in the school where she taught.

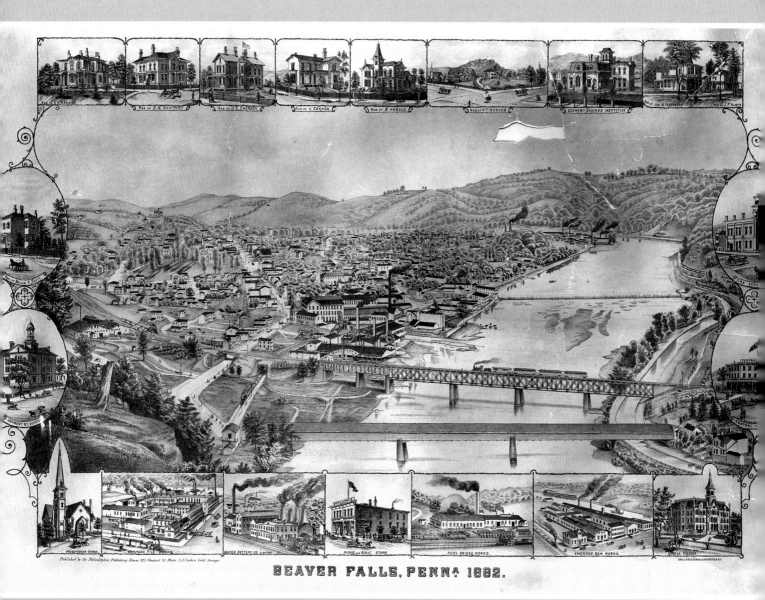

BEAVER FALLS, PENNA 1882.

Beaver Falls in 1882. Note the brand-new college building on the far hill. The original painting is in the collection of the Beaver Falls Historical Museum. This copy of the painting is from the *Beaver County Bicentennial Atlas* and is reprinted by the courtesy of its editor, Denver L. Walton.

THREE

The College on the Hill: Geneva Moves to Beaver Falls

1880 – 1890

"A more desirable location could scarcely be secured. The natural scenery is delightful."

As the enrollment grew, President George saw that Geneva needed a more stable financial base than could be provided even by an increased student body. He therefore set out to raise an endowment for the school, and he met with some success. The campaign for endowment revealed a tension that soon led to the moving of Geneva. The pledges from the Northwood neighborhood were largely made on condition that the college remain in the community; considerably larger pledges came from other areas that wanted the college to move. Those contradictory pledges forced a decision on the college. When the board presented the issue of location to Synod, Synod appointed a carefully chosen committee to consider it. The committee appealed for invitations, and in its report to the 1879 Synod it presented offers from four locations: Northwood; Bellefontaine, nearby in

Ohio; Morning Sun, Iowa; and Beaver Falls, Pennsylvania. The Beaver Falls offer included a promise of land from the Harmony Society and from the

After considering several architects, the committee chose James P. Bailey, of Pittsburgh, who submitted this design for the new college building. He later designed the Butler County Court House, Butler, Pennsylvania, and the First Presbyterian Church in Beaver, Pennsylvania.

community an additional promise of $20,000 for a building. The invitation from Beaver Falls was accepted. Synod appointed a committee to meet in July 1879 to certify that the conditions of the move had been met and, if so, to superintend the move.

How had the proposal from Beaver Falls developed? The Harmony Society, which offered the site, was a group of German pietists living near Beaver Falls in a communal settlement along the Ohio River. Their hard work, the quality of their agricultural and industrial products, and the accessibility of markets had made them prosperous. After the Civil War, they invested their capital in organizing the new town of Beaver Falls at the Middle Falls of the Beaver River. Beaver Falls quickly became a microcosm of the nationwide post-war industrial growth. Many small plants, chiefly in metal-working and clay,

began and prospered, often with the help of Harmonist capital. To encourage the town to grow, the Harmonists offered the college a site on a hill overlooking the

Left: After the original contractor for the college building underbid the job and went bankrupt, William Pearce was persuaded to superintend the construction. He rescued the building committee from financial straits and completed the building. His son, M. M. Pearce, served as the thirteenth president of Geneva. Photo courtesy Kenneth D. Saxton.

Below: This is an early photograph of the college building soon after its erection in 1879–1881.

river and the town. The connection between German pietists and a Reformed Presbyterian college is surprising. Nevertheless, the advantages for both parties were clear. Jacob Henrici, the Harmony Society trustee, was in the process of developing a new industrial town, and a college would enhance the town's prestige and economic prosperity. Henrici could crown his town with a college on the hill. Synod wanted the college moved "East," near large centers of Reformed Presbyterian membership, not rural, but also not too urban. Beaver Falls seemed to fit that description. The local Reformed Presbyterian congregation would be augmented by both faculty and students. It may well have

been a member of that congregation, J. D. McAnlis, who proposed the plan to John Reeves, who was the local agent of the Harmonists.

The committee gathered as directed in the summer of 1879, along with a number of friends, in a grove on the future site of the college. After a picnic dinner the committee convened. John Reeves, for the Harmony Society, formally presented the site to the committee. When it was announced that the $20,000 for the building was not quite met, it was promptly subscribed by those present! The brand-new Pittsburgh and Lake Erie Railroad promised a station at the foot of the hill. With enthusiasm the committee made the move official.

It was agreed that the college would remain in Northwood for the 1879–80 year while the committee was preparing a building in Beaver Falls. That preparation proved frustrating. The building

eventually cost nearly twice the budgeted $20,000 and was not ready for a year after the promised completion date. At the end of the process, the secretary of the committee reported to Synod, "We are free to say that such an undertaking would not have been entered upon if we had been able to see the end from the beginning." Not seeing the future, fortunately, they persevered. Their earnest prayers were answered: the college had an impressive building on a commanding site.

Though the building was not ready for use, the "college" (that is, the library, half the faculty, and some of the students) moved from Northwood to Beaver Falls in the fall of 1880. The trustees filled the vacant chairs of Latin and mathematics. On September 15 the college opened. The editor of *The Cabinet*, the student newspaper, described his feelings after the opening session:

As school adjourned for that day, both Professors and students felt a spirit that they never before so manifested. They seemed to realize that the College had at last found its place. Each one went to his work as if he thought the whole success of the College depended on him.

When they moved from Northwood, Professor and Mrs. McCartney built a house beside the campus and named it Ferncliffe for the wooded cliff on which it stood.

College Avenue was not yet paved in 1890. In the foreground is President George's house, beyond it the house of Greek professor George Kennedy and the mansard roof of the Bole house, built as a private boarding house for students. Note also the new 1888 women's dormitory (later called North Hall).

The building of the Reformed Presbyterian congregation, where classes met the first year in Beaver Falls, still stands at Seventh Avenue and Ninth Street. It is now the home of the Holy Spirit Fellowship Church.

For the first year the students met for classes in the building of the Reformed Presbyterian congregation downtown; they found room and board where they could. President George and Professor McCartney commuted downtown from their lonesome new houses beside the unfinished campus on the college hill.

At the close of that inconvenient year, the first Geneva commencement in Beaver Falls was held outdoors in the spring of 1881 beside the nearly finished building. It was a gala day. The town factories closed. The Pittsburgh and Lake Erie Railroad ran excursion trains, including one bringing the members of Synod, meeting that year in Pittsburgh.

The local newspaper, the *Independent*, reported:

All sorts of vehicles, as well as men, women, and children on foot, might have been seen wending their way to the College campus. The band was playing and people scattered around in all directions were demolishing the contents of innumerable baskets.

After the picnic, the ceremonies began. As usual in those days, the commencement speakers were the students. Each of the five male seniors presented an oration. The lone woman in the class read an essay entitled "Woman." President George made fitting remarks to the seniors and presented their diplomas. The hired band played, appropriately, "We Parted by

The Class of 1881 was the first to graduate in Beaver Falls. The men on the left are J. H. Wylie and James A. Milligan. In the center is William Paxton. On the right are Marshall Boals, R. M. Downie, and Eleanor Hammond Johnston.

the River Side." Then came the dedication of the college building, with an address by James Renwick Willson Sloane, a Geneva president in the 1850s, and by 1881 a professor in the Reformed Presbyterian Seminary and president of the college Board of Trustees. He described the romantic setting of the college, spoke of his hopes for it, and concluded:

Friends of the college and brethren of the Reformed Presbyterian Church, we meet to-day under the most favorable auspices, to dedicate this Institution to sound learning, and to invoke upon its present and its future the blessing of the Covenant God of our fathers.

The college settled comfortably into its new location. The students enjoyed boating on the Beaver River in the summer and skating in the winter. They enjoyed the bustle of the town. They brought baseball fever with them and were soon playing teams from the local factories. They complained vigorously about the muddy walk into town—it was some decades before the town grew to engulf the college. But walk they did—attending church downtown; boarding in town; attending town lectures; and presenting "entertainments" downtown (orations, humorous readings, music) to raise money for college projects. The college promptly attracted a loyal clientele of students from the area. As in Northwood, most of the students at Geneva came from churches of the

---

The college magazine, *The Cabinet*, was begun in Northwood in 1879 and has been published continuously ever since; this is the title page of the first issue published in Beaver Falls. In modern times it has evolved into the student newspaper.

THE COLLEGE CABINET

Vol. III.   BEAVER FALLS, PA., OCTOBER 1880.   No. 1.

The College Cabinet,

THE

GENEVA COLLEGE JOURNAL

SUBSCRIPTION,   - $1.00 PER YEAR.
SINGLE COPIES,   -   -   15 CENTS.
Old subscriptions discontinued after the second number unless otherwise ordered.

CONTENTS.

Baccalaureate Sermon

DELIVERED TO THE CLASS OF '80

PRES. H. H. GEORGE, D. D.

Col. 11, 10. And ye are complete in Him.

Completeness is a word that has scarcely any absolute meaning among men. In its application to human skill and human effort it has a relative meaning. One man having more genius than another is able to complete a piece of mechanism more nearly than the other,

The additions that are made from year to year in the arts of discovery and invention show that in no direction has completeness been attained. Philosophy that has developed the power and process of heat and light and sound—that has shown the many wonders of electricity is yet year by year lifting its stakes of exploration and carrying them farther out into the regions of the unexplored.

The telephone and phonograph and audiphone are but the twilight of a more illustrious midday into which the world is striding. The human intellect is far from having reached the complete limit of its capacity, to trace the lines of God that bind the worlds of space together, or mark out the footprints of Jehovah as these are carved upon the rocks and sands of earth, beyond the line where human intellectual foot has trod, innumerable worlds stretch out afar, and beneath its farthest ken, God still unfolds himself in ways of wisdom wonderful.

Morally and spiritually our race is as the infant creeping upon the floor, we have not yet reached maturity, much less have we at-

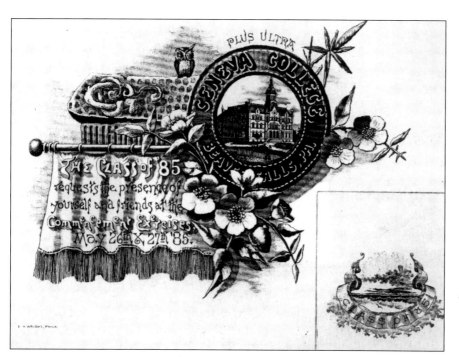

"The presence of yourself and friends." In 1885, as now, graduates invited their friends to share in their important day.

Below: For many years each graduate spoke at commencement. Classes for seniors ended some weeks before graduation to allow them time to prepare their presentations. The men memorized and delivered original orations; the women read their essays. This 1885 program lists the names of the seniors and their topics.

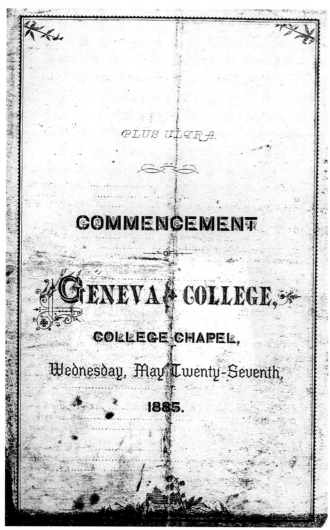

PLUS ULTRA.

COMMENCEMENT

OF

GENEVA COLLEGE,

COLLEGE CHAPEL,

Wednesday, May Twenty-Seventh,

1885.

ORDER OF EXERCISES.

At 10:30 A. M.

MUSIC.

PRAYER.

MUSIC.

SALUTATORY,—"The Pictured Windows."...................Mary A. Benham.

ORATION,—"Head and Hand."........................Samuel G. Connor.

ORATION,—"The Influence of an Ideal."...................John C. Crofts.

MUSIC.

ORATION.—"Education the True Principle of Reform."...........Wm. S. Grim.

ORATION,—"Political Reconstruction."......................Jos. L. Hunter.

ORATION,—"Self Culture."..........................Geo. R. McBurney.

ORATION,—"The American Citizen.".....................Fred J. Nannah.

MUSIC.

ORATION,—"A Model."................................R. C. Reed.

ORATION,—"Mutation.".........................W. Lloyd C. Samson.

ESSAY,—"Seekers.".................................Jennie M. Slater.

MUSIC.

At 2:30 P. M.

ORATION,—"Character in Politics.".................J. Lawrence Autenreith.

ORATION,—"Social Evolution.".........................J. M. Crowe.

ORATION,—"Conflicting Forces.".........................J. A. Greer.

MUSIC.

ESSAY,—"Great Names not all.".......................Anna R. Patterson.

ORATION,—"Capacity."..............................John B. Steel.

ORATION,—"Environment.".........................John S. Thompson.

MUSIC.

ESSAY,—"Individual Capabilities.".....................Etta H. Thompson.

ORATION,—"Liberty and Law." ....John B White

ORATION,—"Our Inheritance and Bequest."...............J. S. Wilson.

MUSIC.

VALEDICTORY ORATION..............................J Knox Reed.

Presbyterian family, and it was with such congregations that the college for some time had its closest associations.

The basic curriculum of the college changed little from the Northwood days, although there was intense curricular dispute in the old Eastern colleges. The dispute was precipitated when Harvard abandoned the traditional single curriculum to offer students a total choice of electives. Like most small colleges, Geneva stayed with tradition. President George, himself the product of a classical education and Geneva's professor of Greek, defended keeping Greek at the center of the curriculum:

The student must be wanting in ability or taste who cannot find both discipline and valuable information in studying the rich language and thoughts of our most influential intellectual ancestors, the people of ancient Greece. . . . The literature of ancient Greece is so original and so complete in its varieties that, if literature be worth studying at all, it will be found that no other people have created and can present such an orderly development of epic, lyric, dramatic, oratorical, historical and critical work.

In other ways Geneva was not traditional. Two significant additions to the curriculum, unique to Geneva, were made during this decade. When a position on the faculty was created for David McAllister in 1880, it was to include courses in Bible and in political science as part of the required curriculum. Courses in the Bible had not been part of the American college curriculum, even in denominational colleges. Perhaps it was assumed that Bible courses were unnecessary for students who largely came from homes where they had memorized the catechism and Bible verses and who at college attended daily chapel. McAllister intended to teach Bible as a college-level course, dealing with the history of Bible times, the

Right: Professor David McAllister was appointed to the faculty to teach courses in Bible and in political science. Both of these subjects were innovations in a college curriculum.

This early recruitment effort describes the college in its new location and the curriculum it offers.

GENEVA COLLEGE.

Beaver   Falls, Pa.

GENEVA COLLEGE

A BEAUTIFUL Stone Building situated on the Beaver River, with a large and spacious campus, and attractive surroundings. Ample facilities for boarding near the college at the lowest rates. Club boarding as low as $2.50 per week. There are

TWO COMPLETE COLLEGE COURSES,

Classical and Scientific, in which students are graduated with the college degree of A. B. or B. S.

There is besides an Eclectic Course adapted to the particular needs of any student. Two preparatory years admitting students from the beginning of the course, both male and female.

MUSIC, VOCAL AND INSTRUMENTAL

Is taught in the college by a competent instructor. Hebrew and German belong to the regular course. Special attention is given to the

SCIENCE OF CIVIL GOVERNMENT.

The College occupies the highest and most advanced ground in this department, applying a sound Christian political philosophy to all the public questions of the day, such as Temperance, the Sabbath, Marriage and Divorce, State Education, &c.

With our present and increasing facilities we can guarantee an exceptionally thorough preparation of our students for the duties and responsibilities of public life. Our Library was increased last year with books to the amount of over $1,200.

Our students have increased in number from year to year, and the outlook for the coming year is very encouraging.

THE FALL SESSION OPENS SEPTEMBER 3.

It is important that students be present promptly at the opening.

Catalogues furnished and full information given on application to the president,   H. H. GEORGE, D. D.

Please read, and extend the information to any who may have children to educate.

The contests of the Adelphic and Aletheorian Literary Societies, suspended in Northwood because of the intense rivalry, were revived in Beaver Falls in 1884. In that contest the Adelphic Society was victorious.

geographic setting of the Bible, and the doctrinal content of the Scripture. Ever since, courses in Bible have been required of all Geneva graduates.

The other unique addition to the curriculum was in political science. Few colleges offered courses in political science in the 1880s, and in none were they required. The motivation for this addition was the long-standing concern of Reformed Presbyterians over the nature of government, specifically that the American constitution was a secular document, without reference to God. This, they believed, dishonored Jesus Christ, whom the Bible calls the King of kings and the Lord of lords. During the Civil War, the National Reform Association was organized by people of many denominations to work for a "Christian" amendment to the constitution. McAllister had been a leader in that enterprise and he was invited to Geneva to make sure that the curriculum would include serious academic consideration of this central concern. One year of political science was required of all seniors: one term in which McAllister related the biblical teaching about the sovereignty of

God to his extensive study of political theory; one term studying American government (a subject almost nowhere taught at that time); and one term devoted to international relations. This unique concern of Geneva was the occasion for its choice of motto, *Pro Christo et Patria* (For Christ and Country), adopted in 1881. McAllister was a pioneer in the integration of faith and learning. His presentation of Christian truth (as he understood it) was not isolated from the long history of political theory. His presentation of political theory and practice was in the light of his commitment to the Bible.

The treasurer of the Board of Trustees reported expenditures of $4,234.24 for the first year after the move. Of that, 92 percent went for faculty salaries, leaving $331 for other expenses. The total college budget was somewhat larger: there was also a faculty treasurer who collected tuition and fees, and who paid some college expenses before sending the rest of the tuition to the treasurer of the board. There was, of course, no money for supporting staff. The faculty did everything, from collecting student tuition to planting trees on the campus.

At least twice there have been suggestions for amending the motto of the college. The first came in the period after World War II, when Americans were moving away from their long isolationism. It was proposed that the words *et Mundo* be added to the motto: For Christ, the Country, and the World. The second came in the 1970s when some Christians seemed almost to equate America with the Kingdom of God. In protest *The Cabinet* dropped the words *et Patria* from its masthead—For Christ! Neither of these suggestions prevailed.

As a result some desirable things did not get done. For example, the library. One professor was named librarian: *The Cabinet* complained that the library was not open during class hours! The president, in addition to his teaching, administrative duties, and fund raising, was in charge of the building and grounds. Understandably that latter function got short shrift: *The Cabinet* editorialized about dirty halls and the pile of cinders at the back door. That highly visible problem led to the employment of a janitor, about 1883, creating the first staff position at Geneva (a reminder of how important a function the Buildings and Grounds staff performs). Twenty-five years later another staff position was created, this time for the library.

When there were unbudgeted needs, the board appointed a committee to raise the funds. There were no seats in the chapel for the first year; a Furnishings Committee was named to provide chairs in time for the 1882 commencement. When McAllister began his course, textbooks in political science did not

Solomon Ford Kingston, a noted athlete and a talented entertainer, was a favorite with his fellow students. After graduation from seminary he was pastor of the Reformed Presbyterian congregation in Selma, Alabama.

"Our ball team received their suits last Saturday. They certainly are dandies." The baseball team in 1884 (or 1885) posed for its picture in the new uniforms. Back row, left to right: John B. Steel, '85; unknown; G. P. Emery, '87; S. Cargill Milligan, '88; W. L. C. Samson, '85. Front row, left to right: unknown; Solomon Ford Kingston, '85; J. H. Kennedy, '86; William Charlton; J. R. Wylie '87.

exist. He lectured, and soon asked for desks in place of benches so that the students could take notes. This request was also referred to the Furnishings Committee. The music teacher raised funds for a piano. Science teachers raised money for laboratory equipment and a telescope. The faculty collectively raised money for the first gymnasium.

The first addition to the campus after the original college building was a dormitory in the late 1880s. President George recognized that a place on the campus where the women could have rooms and where students could eat their meals would make attending Geneva more attractive. *The Cabinet* lent its editorial support to the project. However, with substantial capital campaigns for the college building and for the endowment just completed, the timing was bad. Proposals for financing the dormitory were suggested and discarded. At length, in some desperation, a number of friends of the college formed The Geneva Company Limited. They took enough shares to raise $4,000 toward the $8,000 cost of the building and borrowed the remainder. The dormitory was erected along College Avenue just north of the college building and opened for the spring term of 1888. At once, of course, there began to appear in *The Cabinet* remarks about dormitory food and the forced seclusion of the women. *The Cabinet*, with the irony common to college students of any generation, proposed that for the safety of the women in case of fire, each room should have its own fire escape!

Chapel services were an integral

The Geneva Company published regulations for the new dormitory. Mrs. Dodds, the first matron, was the widow of the pioneer Reformed Presbyterian missionary to Syria.

part of the college day, as they had been in Northwood, and for many years they came first in the schedule. The weekly prayer meeting continued, voluntary and student-run. Because it was a two-mile walk to town, the college began its own worship services on the Lord's Day. Professor W. P. Johnston, with his gentle concern for the spiritual life of the students, was chosen college pastor to preach on alternate Sabbaths and granted a modest stipend for his service. The other ministerial members of the faculty shared the responsibility for preaching.

The students quickly reorganized their literary societies in Beaver Falls. The architect had designed the college building with a pair of handsome rooms for them on the third floor, which they furnished elegantly. As in Northwood, much of the campus social life centered around their Friday meetings; practice in writing, speaking, and engagement with the issues of the day contributed to the intellectual life of the college.

During the first spring in Beaver Falls, a pickup baseball team played the File Works Club twice, each team winning a game. By 1884, a more formal team was established, with uniforms provided by a student association. Geneva teams defeated Washington & Jefferson College and the University of Pittsburgh, as well as local teams. By 1888, Geneva's teams were playing on a

In 1888, a second building was added to the campus to provide housing for women and a place where students could take their meals. Friends of the college organized The Geneva Company to erect and operate it; later it became the property of the college.

"The ladies' lawn-tennis club of Geneva will play the ladies' lawn tennis club of Beaver Falls a series of games this spring." *The Cabinet,* March 1886. A photograph of the tennis team about 1890. Back row: Elizabeth Kennedy (Goehring), Mary Garrett, Margaret George. Front row: Tillie Witherspoon (Gilmore), Mame George (McCarroll), Wilhelmina McCartney (Guerard).

The turnstile at the College Avenue entrance kept wandering cows off the campus.

rented field named Geneva Park at the corner of College Avenue and 27th Street. (For many years this land was occupied by an Armstrong Cork Company plant; only recently has it returned to its original use as part of the Merriman Sports Complex.)

In the fall of 1889, President George told the Board of Trustees of his intention to retire the next year. The board accepted his resignation, reporting to the Synod of 1890:

Contrasting the present condition and prospects of the college . . . with what these were eighteen years ago, when, at the call of the Synod, he took charge of the institution, . . . the board felt it due to place on the records a warm and unstinted testimonial to his efficient leadership in securing these happy

results. His name is so interwoven with the struggles of the past that it cannot be separated from the achievements of the future; and whatever noble mission Geneva College may yet fulfil, it should not be forgotten that it owes much of the possibilities of its future to its now retiring president.

He did not retire to inactivity. He served as a pastor and on the staffs of the American Sabbath Union and the National Reform Association until his death in 1914. To succeed him as president the board chose William Pollock Johnston, professor of English literature and college pastor. He was a nephew of the founder, John Black Johnston, the third in his family to serve as president of Geneva.

Left: This room, on the second floor of the college building, served as chapel, auditorium, and general gathering place for college activities. One Halloween all the chairs disappeared and were located on the college roof.

Below: These stanzas are from a bit of verse entitled "The College Bell," published in the *The Cabinet* for October 1897.

The belfry acquired a bell in the fall of 1883. It was rung at 6:00 a.m. to wake the students in the nearby boarding houses; again at 8:00 a.m. for chapel; and through the day for classes. It was also rung to celebrate college victories. By the next February the clapper was stolen, creating a tradition that endured for decades. The 1937 *Genevan*.

When you hurry toward the college,
In the fear of being late;
When you just have gotten courage,
That perhaps it's not your fate:
Then you hear the bell a ringing
And its very like a knell,
For you know you'll get a scolding,
When you hear the "college bell."

When moist with perspiration,
When in class your turn is nigh,
When you fear a recitation,
When your tongue and lips are dry,
When the minutes have no fleetness,
Then it sounds not like a knell,
For there's music and there's sweetness
In the welcome "college bell."

When you haven't got your lesson,
And the " 'fessor" calls on you,
When you know you'll make a mess of
Everything you try to do;
When he just has asked a sticker
Which he's wanting you to tell;
Then it makes you almost snicker,
When you hear the "college bell."

When the boys are playing football
And your're sitting in your room;
When you think the boys are beaten,
That they've surely met their doom;
Then you hear an awful ringing,
And you give the college yell,
For you know the boys have "flymed 'em
When you hear the "college bell."

President William Pollock Johnston

William Pollock Johnston (1839–1920) was president of Geneva for seventeen years, from 1890 to 1907. He attended Geneva but received his degree from Jefferson College in 1858. After serving Reformed Presbyterian pastorates in Baltimore and in Washington, Iowa, he came to Geneva in 1881 as professor of Latin and English literature. He was named president emeritus in 1907. Until his death in 1920, he was a familiar and beloved figure on the campus.

FOUR

GROWING PROFESSIONALISM

1890 — 1916

The first college basketball game in the United States was played at Geneva on April 8, 1893, when Geneva defeated the New Brighton YMCA.

The 1890s were a stable period in the history of Geneva. The college changed, in some ways very significantly, but without crisis. The qualifications and preparation for college professors were changing. Faculty members were less likely to be new college graduates who "heard classes." William M. Milroy, who succeeded to the Latin chair when Johnston became president, came to Geneva from graduate school at Johns Hopkins University and in 1891 became the first Ph.D. on the Geneva faculty. James M. Coleman came to the chair of political philosophy in 1892 after two years of graduate study at the University of Michigan, later supplemented at the universities of Wisconsin and Chicago, and in Germany.

The physical sciences grew in significance in the curriculum. The bachelor of science degree became a four-year course with more science and mathematics and was made equivalent in prestige to the bachelor of arts degree. Johnston left his physical mark on the campus by proposing a separate building for the sciences and by raising the funds to erect it. The Science Hall

was completed in 1897, a further symbol of the importance the sciences were taking in the life of Geneva. That building was destroyed by fire in 1912 and rebuilt on the same foundation. Later it was gradually expanded along the hill and became the Science and Engineering Building.

From the time Geneva moved to Beaver Falls, *The Cabinet* had been agitating for a building in which students could exercise. There were rowing and

The Science Hall, built in 1897, was a special project of President Johnston. It was both a handsome addition to the campus and a reminder of the increasing importance of science in the college curriculum.

skating on the river, of course, and there were baseball games; but students needed a place for regular physical activity, for their health and as an outlet for energies after sitting at the books. Gymnasiums had recently appeared on college campuses, not for sports, but for physical training, as the country became conscious of the value of exercise in maintaining health. The Geneva faculty responded to student needs by raising funds to build a gymnasium, a small frame building, completed in the fall of 1890 and located at what was then the northeast corner of the campus.

The trustees staffed the gymnasium by employing C. O. Bemies, a graduate of the new Physical Training Department of the YMCA Training School in Springfield, Massachusetts, offering him a modest stipend and free tuition as he completed his college study. He put the gym to use at once, offering a class for boys from four to five each afternoon and for girls from five to six; activities were organized to be fun as well as useful, consisting of games, drills, and calisthenics.

Top Left: With the building of the gymnasium, Charles O. Bemies was employed to provide physical training exercises in it. He brought football, basketball, and the YMCA to Geneva.

The first gymnasium was built in 1890, located near what was then the northeast corner of the campus. It was razed about 1910 for the building of Johnston Gymnasium.

Along with his professional commitment to physical education, Bemies was also greatly interested in team sports. In the autumn of 1890, he organized Geneva's first football team, with himself at halfback. After a minimum of practice the team set off for Pittsburgh to play the Western University of Pennsylvania (now the University of Pittsburgh)—and lost 10-4. The next fall, 1891, was Geneva's first full season. With Bemies still at halfback, the team played six games and won four, defeating W.U.P twice, 12-4 and 6-4, and winning a victory over Westminster College, 42-0! (Geneva's defeat of Westminster was especially sweet. The long athletic rivalry between the two schools had already begun with baseball games in the 1880s, shortly after Geneva moved to Beaver Falls.) In the spring of 1891, Bemies reorganized the baseball team, which had been active during the 1880s but had languished. The same spring he trained the Geneva track men well enough that the college placed second in a regional track meet, after Washington and Jefferson College.

Geneva is especially indebted to Bemies and the YMCA for the introduction of basketball, a new game just developed in 1891 by James Naismith at the YMCA Training School. Basketball at once became a popular indoor game for winter. *The Cabinet* noted, "It suits very well to take the place of football for those who love a rough and tumble game." The first college basketball game in the United States was played at Geneva on April 8, 1893, when Geneva defeated the New Brighton YMCA. Though he stayed at Geneva only four years before going off to seminary, Bemies made a significant impact on the history of physical education and athletics at Geneva, an impact that would be hard to overestimate.

Bemies also had a strategic impact on the spiritual life of the campus. In 1890, the YMCA was a strongly evangelical and evangelistic organization. Coming from the YMCA Training School, he quickly organized a YMCA at Geneva, then a YWCA. There were weekly meetings, with a schedule of daily Bible reading and prayer, and there was a concern to encourage students who had made no profession of faith in Christ to do so. These organizations stimulated an interest in missions, both overseas and at home. They sponsored at least three Bible schools, meeting on Sabbath afternoons in unchurched neighborhoods. At YMCA, YWCA, and Student Volunteer Movement conferences, students had contacts with Christian students on other campuses. Through Bemies's emphasis on personal commitment to Christ, students found a faith once taken for granted now becoming more personal and more vital.

In recognition of his services to Geneva, he was honored in 1917 with the degree of Doctor of Divinity.

Once football began under Bemies, the college took to it with enthusiasm. In 1894, the team, captained by R. H. Martin, was undefeated, outscoring their opponents 108-8. With such a record the college clearly needed its own field. The original ten acres had provided a handsome site for the college building, but no level ground for athletics. To replace the rented field at the foot of the hill, Johnston purchased ground across College Hill, endearing himself both to the athletes and the fans. That 33rd Street field was *the* college field until Reeves Stadium was opened for football

in 1925. The first game, on October 10, 1896, was played before a large crowd against Geneva's nemesis, Washington and Jefferson. Geneva lost 34-0. The next week, however, Geneva won its game against Grove City College 32-0 and went on to defeat Westminster 18-4. By the turn of the century, in the years 1900–1903, Coach J. B. Craig compiled

Left: The 1901 football team, coached by J. B. Craig, had a record of 5-1-2. The members of the team were J. M. May, hb; J. L. Walkinshaw, le; D. B. Martin, lt; S. G. Finney, rh; P. T. Barnes, lg; A. McKean, c; J. C. Edgar, rg; A. W. Leech, rt; P. N. Critchlow, re; J. H. Thompson, lt; W. G. East, rt; J. R. George, fb; R. H. George, qb; W. M. Robb, le; W. T. Levis, fb.

Below: Geneva fans are standing at the ticket window of the 33rd Street field. The ground was purchased by President Johnston in 1896 to provide a level athletic field for the college as its sports program grew.

a 26-3-3 record, the best football record in Geneva's history. Basketball, which Bemies had introduced to Geneva in 1893, became an intercollegiate sport in 1897. Early success came under Coach Joe Thompson, who compiled a 28-14 record from 1898 to 1902.

The management and funding of the athletic program was in student hands. With the arrival of football in 1890, the Geneva Athletic Association solicited contributions to set up goal posts on the rented field and to provide uniforms and gear for the team. The constitution of the association, adopted in 1893, provided that the association would choose the manager of the team, who would be responsible for scheduling games and paying expenses; that the team would choose its own captain; that funding for the program would come from membership dues and gate receipts. When the students fenced the new field in 1897, the association organized an "entertainment" to pay for it.

A decade later the sports program was the center of a very emotional crisis on the campus. As the twentieth century

By faculty action in the spring of 1906, football was abolished as an intercollegiate sport. The decision caused consternation on the campus. Students held the mock funeral pictured here. The faculty reversed its action the next spring.

Gold and White have been Geneva's colors since at least 1891. By the time Vale Downie wrote this ode to them in 1901, they had been covered with athletic glory:

For the White and Gold
Gen-e-va! Gen-e-va!
The trial is almost done;
And see the score, a minute more
Play, and the game is won.
The cheers have died on every side
For crowds are waiting breathless:
Win out the game and leave your fame
Where time will find it deathless.
Hard! Hard! Hard! Hard!
For the game's to the strong and bold,
  And we'll tell the might
  At the fire tonight,
Of your deeds for the white and gold.

began, the football team under Coach J. B. Craig had a series of winning seasons: 5-1-1 in 1900, 5-1-2 in 1901, 7-0 in 1902, and 9-1 in 1903. In the two years 1902 and 1903, only eight points were scored against Geneva. Football fever ran high. But across the country football was coming under increasing criticism. There were few rules protecting players and it was a dangerous game. There were no standards for eligibility and colleges were openly paying players to play. Within the Reformed Presbyterian Church, some members saw devotion to sports as a substitute for devotion to the Kingdom of God. The editor of a church magazine wrote, "We have heard of 'the Geneva Nines'; we would like to hear of the Geneva students' mission bands." With this spreading opposition to football—and after two losing seasons in 1904 and 1905—the faculty decided to end football as a college sport beginning with the 1906 season. Unfortunately President Johnston was not on campus to deal with the crisis, having been directed by the trustees to spend the year traveling to raise endowment funds. And

Right: When President Emeritus Johnston died in 1920, the *Genevan* of that year was dedicated to his memory. The art editor for the yearbook, John Steuart Curry, did this portrait.

Below: The hall of the Adelphic Society pictured here was on the third floor of the college building (Old Main). The Aletheorian Society had a comparable hall down the corridor. The societies were responsible for decorating and furnishing their halls. (The offices of the Department of Business, Accounting, and Management now occupy that space.)

crisis it was. The disappearance of football was the major topic on campus: student morale dropped, enrollment dropped, relations with the sports-minded community were strained. After a tense fall and winter, the faculty reversed itself, bowing to student opinion and noting that opponents of football in the denomination had not increased their support when it was outlawed. There would again be football in the fall!

Although it made the editorial columns of *The Cabinet* less frequently, a more far-reaching crisis was developing at the same time that the football issue erupted. For some time, the college had been accumulating a steadily larger overdraft in their account with the denominational treasurer. Finally forced to face the problem, the Board of Trustees appointed a committee "to consider the whole condition of the college as to finances." As the scope of that inquiry broadened (finances are rarely the only problem), Johnston was named president emeritus and asked to continue his work in fundraising and recruitment; changes were made in the

membership of the board; and William Henry George was elected president.

The new president was the son of President H. H. George, who had revived the college in 1872 and presided over its move to Beaver Falls. At the time of his election the younger George was twenty-eight years old and pastor of the Vernon, Wisconsin, Reformed Presbyterian congregation. He had studied at Harvard and Princeton Universities and was the first Geneva president to have done graduate work other than at seminary. He brought to the president's office a different concept of a college education, and during his nine-year presidency Geneva changed rapidly.

George was concerned that faculty members be people of "scholarly instincts and ambitions." He encouraged Geneva professors to take leaves of absence for graduate study, though he recognized the costs both to them and to the college whose resources were stretched by their absence. He set an example by spending the year 1911–1912 on leave at Harvard. During his presidency, five members of a small faculty took year-long leaves for graduate study, at

Harvard, at the exciting new University of Chicago, or by study abroad. In addition, most faculty members spent their summers at universities.

George believed strongly that teachers should teach, not just "hear classes." He recognized a role for the lecture "by a scholar who has mastered the material on his own"; but he also believed that "in a small college too much is done for a student, not enough by him." Thus he favored informal discussion in small groups, collateral reading and reports, the study of cases in a course such as international law. He looked forward to a schedule in which classes would not meet every day of the week, allowing time for individual work.

George presided over the demise of the "preps." From the beginning, like almost every other college, Geneva had had a preparatory department. Students came to Geneva from the common schools, where they had learned the "three R's." If in the entrance examination they could demonstrate that they were prepared, they would be admitted to what was called the Academic Department. For two years (later three or four), they would study Latin, English grammar, more mathematics, some history, on their way to becoming college freshmen. Many students therefore came onto the college campus when they were fourteen or fifteen (and amused or annoyed their more sophisticated elders). Other students came late, farm boys deciding they wanted to prepare for college. Usually there were more "preps" than college students. It must have been an interesting mix.

In the days before public high schools were common, preparatory departments served a necessary function for the students and were useful for the college, allowing it to control standards for admission to college work and helping recruit students. As public high schools became available, however, the need for the Academic Department diminished. Enrollments in it at Geneva were dropping rapidly, by 1912 down to twenty-eight students. The Board of Trustees approved the president's recommendation that the Academic Department be ended in 1912, with a "sub-freshman year" during 1912–1913 as a transition. The move was generally applauded, and to the president's joy the college could behave more like a college.

George's concern for scholarship was appropriately timed. Nationally there was a growing concern to find objective ways for measuring the quality of a college. College founding had been a very *laissez-faire* process in the United States. Charters were granted freely; anyone who wanted to establish a college could try. Many such trials failed, and the colleges that survived varied greatly in entrance requirements and degree programs. Let the buyer (i.e. the prospective student—or parent) beware! How could the quality of a college be measured?

In his annual report to the trustees in 1913, President George noted a number of ways in which Geneva's quality was being recognized. The Supreme Court of Pennsylvania accepted a Geneva diploma in lieu of an examination in the registration of law students. The Superintendent of Instruction in Pennsylvania granted certification for teaching on the basis of a Geneva degree. Geneva was on the accredited list at Columbia University. But George also summarized a report of the United States Office of Education which divided colleges into four classes based on quantitative measures, such as the teaching load of department chairmen, the number of academic departments, the standards for faculty, the value of laboratory equipment, the size of the library and of the endowment. On the basis of those quantitative measures, Geneva would rank in Class B or C.

"It behooves us," George said, "to ask ourselves where we stand, for whatever we may think of such classifications our graduates will meet them at every turn. . . ." He warned the board against the danger of combining departments, scaling down appropriations, lowering salaries, increasing work loads: "The danger lies in dropping our college into a lower class until we shall be rated as a . . . collegiate institute [Class D]." He concluded on a more hopeful note:

It is my firm conviction that in the spirit and tone of the school, in efficiency of instruction, in character of the curriculum, in conservatism in granting honorary degrees, and in all other points called qualitative standards that Geneva stands in Class A. And in the quantitative standards she ought to stand in Class B.

Along with his concern for scholarship, George was determined that the college become more of a presence in the Beaver Valley. One of his maxims was that if the college was to receive, it must give. That is, if Geneva hoped for community support it must meet needs existing in the community. Under his leadership, the curriculum was broadened to include a third course called, curiously enough, Latin Scientific. The course led to the B.A. degree, which many students desired, but without the hurdle of four years of Greek, which seemed of little purpose in the callings they were pursuing. Latin-Scientific became a popular program.

Another growing need in the community was for training teachers, as standards for teaching in the public schools were being raised. George tried an interesting experiment: in 1908 he moved the whole college calendar two weeks later, so that the spring term would begin after the rural schools in the county had closed. This allowed teachers to enroll in it, and special classes were offered for them. In 1909, thirty-two teachers attended. For some years a summer school for teachers had been operated by a group of local educators in the college building. At George's suggestion, the college assumed responsibility for it in 1908, and in 1912 the spring term for teachers was merged with it. To coordinate these programs, the college established a Department of Education in 1908, and in 1909 George brought H. H. Wylie to head the department and to teach psychology.

Until his untimely death in 1923, Wylie was a major influence on the Geneva campus. He developed an effective and recognized program for training teachers, shepherded the new summer school and made it work, and began the Extension Program which helped a growing number of area students achieve a college education. Wylie had a deep personal influence on Geneva students. He involved himself energetically in student activities: he taught a Bible class each Sabbath morning before the worship service, started a Debate Club for intercollegiate

debates, and organized a men's glee club which made an annual tour advertising the college.

Under President George, music and oratory were expanded and an art department added. These departments were patronized by people in town as well as by college students, for lessons in music, elocution, and art. They contributed greatly to the cultural life of the campus, presenting recitals in music and speech, and providing music and declamations for many college functions. The Department of Oratory (later Public Speaking) presented plays, ranging from amusing farces to Shakespeare and the provocative contemporary dramas of Ibsen and Shaw. The relationship of these departments to the college was curious both financially and academically. The teachers were expected to support themselves by the fees they charged for lessons, besides returning a percentage of those fees to the college; thus they operated outside the college budget (and subsidized it) while adding to the life of the school. College credit was not given for classes taken in these areas; but students who completed the courses pre-

The William Pollock Johnston Gymnasium was dedicated in 1911, replacing the original wooden gymnasium of 1890.

scribed were granted Geneva degrees in their appropriate fields: Bachelor of Music, Bachelor of Oratory, or a certificate in art. (The first three women to finish the prescribed course in music, in 1891, were awarded the degree of Mistress of Music.)

Since the early 1880s, a janitor had been the only staff person aiding the faculty. Under George, two important positions were added. In 1907, Berdella

President George is conversing with Robert Clarke. Dr. Clarke was named to the staff of the college in 1909, primarily to be a fundraiser. He was responsible for the construction of Johnston Gymnasium, McKee Hall, Reeves Field, and McCartney Library. In countless other ways he served the college until his retirement in 1958. His son, Edwin C. Clarke, became the fifteenth president of Geneva. Photograph courtesy Marshall W. Smith.

Walker was employed as secretary to the president and as librarian. To make this arrangement possible, the library was

THE NEW GYMNASIUM
June 6, 1911

No more the pale-faced, blear-eyed, brain-fagged youth,
With shoulders stooped and frame by bookish toil unstrung.
Health's Temple now is reared upon our heights;
Gymnastic twists and feats will now correct
The maladies of thought and offset all its waste.
Hail to the Gym! to all its merry donors, thanks.

(from an ode by George Kennedy, Professor of Greek)

moved to a room next to the president's office. Miss Walker's employment was a major step forward in the role of the library; it was now open most of the day and available for students to use. The use of the library and the circulation of books increased rapidly, and there were no more complaints that the library was closed. The president continued to handle his personal correspondence; the secretary was responsible for answering the new telephone in his office and for mailing out catalogues and brochures publicizing the offerings of the college.

In 1909, George asked the trustees to appoint a third staff person to be a fundraiser. At once Robert Clarke came to wear many hats around the college. A man of energy, persuasiveness, and taste, he played a large role in the life of Geneva. As a fundraiser he was impressive, reporting pledges of $27,000 in his first six months (the annual budget in 1908 was less than $20,000). The board expressed its "hearty appreciation," and responded to his success by assigning him the following responsibilities during the next year:

Seek funds for a new gymnasium, cement walks for the entire college, and an addition to the dormitory;

Call the attention of friends of the college to the need for a recital hall for the Department of Music;

Communicate with John Reeves, Sr., about a gift of land along College Avenue;

Ask Mr. Underwood for typewriters;

Spend a month in recruiting students;

Find local businessmen who would serve as consultative members of the board, and Approach Synod's Board of Trustees about a construction loan for a gymnasium.

Two years later, the Board of Trustees adopted a formal job description, but it was hardly a protection: to raise funds as his principal work; to collect tuition from the students,

replacing a faculty treasurer; to be responsible for all repair work, purchasing supplies, and paying bills; and to "carry out in conjunction with the president any arrangements into which they may enter in the interests of the college."

One of Clarke's assignments was to increase the endowment. Some years earlier, when the endowment stood at about $140,000, Andrew Carnegie had promised that if the college would raise $45,000 toward the endowment, he would contribute the last $15,000 to make it an even $200,000. President Johnston had set out to raise the $45,000, had quickly gotten pledges up to that amount, and approached Carnegie for the $15,000. But the philanthropist, being a canny Scotsman, knew that pledges and cash were not the same and demanded either cash or dependable notes before fulfilling his promise. Clarke was able to satisfy Carnegie and the promised $15,000 appeared.

Another of Clarke's projects was the provision of a more adequate gymnasium to accommodate the growing athletic program of the college. Clarke raised the money and the new gymnasium was built. Its architect was William G. Eckles, of New Castle, who later designed McKee Hall and McCartney Library. The gymnasium was dedicated during commencement week in 1911 and appropriately named in honor of President Emeritus William Pollock Johnston, who had enthusiastically presided over the growth of Geneva's athletic program. Bemies returned for the occasion.

In the next two years, both Clarke's optimism and his fundraising abilities were severely tested. In 1912, the Science Hall burned; and the next spring a tornado took much of the roof off Old Main (as the original college building came to be called), severely damaging the chapel. In both cases he was able to

Sometime during the 1890s Geneva students began singing the Alma Mater of Union College, replacing the "Mohawk vale" with the "Beaver vale." By 1910, at least, it had become the official Geneva Alma Mater, as well.

In the spring of 1914, a tornado took the roof off Old Main and severely damaged the chapel. Under Robert Clarke's direction the chapel was extensively remodeled. The stained glass windows now in the chapel were installed, with the seals of Oxford and Cambridge Universities and the Geneva seal pictured in them.

This recitation room in the rebuilt Science Hall, pictured about 1916, was used for chemistry, biology, and geology classes. Photograph courtesy Marshall W. Smith.

Below: The college community was shocked when the Science Hall was destroyed by fire in the spring of 1912. From the Downie Collection.

The Science Hall was rebuilt on the same site. It had a less interesting roof line but was as fireproof as possible and more conveniently arranged than the original building.

The college dining room was on the ground floor of the women's dormitory. From the Downie Collection.

Professor Kennedy, who taught Greek, was an avid photographer. Presumably he took this photograph of a faculty picnic—his wife is pictured but he is not. Left to right in the front row: Miss McClintock (French and German), Mrs. Kennedy, Mrs. Colwell (who as Della Walker had served as librarian from 1907 until her marriage in 1911), President George, Mr. Patton (chemistry), Miss McDowell (English), Miss Jamison (librarian). In the back row, Professor McIsaac (history), Professor Colwell (physics), and Miss Keir (art).

The women's dormitory of 1888 was remodeled in 1905 (the side porch) and 1912 (a new front porch). This is a later picture, taken probably after it was renamed North Hall and became a men's dormitory.

secure funds for repairs, and in both cases good came out of disaster. The Science Hall was rebuilt, with concrete floors and as fireproof as possible, with its rooms more conveniently arranged. The unroofing of the chapel was the occasion for a much-needed remodeling. Again Clarke's taste came into its own: the stage was reconstructed, a sloping floor added, the awkward balcony redesigned, and electric lights installed. The two rows of windows were replaced by tall windows with the seals of Geneva College and of the Universities of Oxford and Cambridge in their stained glass, the gift of Rev. Charles Bell, Class of 1895, and his wife, Ellen Johnston Bell, a niece of three Johnston presidents.

About the turn of the century, six western Pennsylvania colleges organized an Intercollegiate Oratorical Association to sponsor an annual contest. There was vigorous competition at Geneva for the honor of representing the college, and Geneva did well in intercollegiate competition. In 1913 and 1914, Geneva took second place, then first place for four successive years. Intercollegiate debate at Geneva began informally in a debate with Westminster in 1908, which Geneva won. When H. H. Wylie joined the faculty, he organized a debate team. They debated serious topics: the commission form of government for cities; the Monroe Doctrine; the municipal takeover of street railways. Geneva's record was

President George leads a commencement procession across the campus to Old Main.

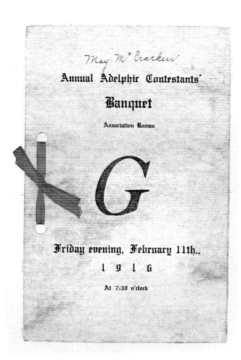
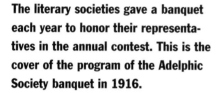

The literary societies gave a banquet each year to honor their representatives in the annual contest. This is the cover of the program of the Adelphic Society banquet in 1916.

The Adelphic contestants in 1916 were Charles Boots, Wilbur Weir, Elizabeth Ewing (later Mrs. Wilbur Weir), Melville Carson, Lola Weir. The Adelphic Society was the victor in this contest 8-2.

[When President George (?) Got Excited]

The Cabinet, April 1915

At eleven o'clock on the night of the Westminster debate our ancient brazen emblem of times and seasons startled the neighborhood by emitting a series of whole-hearted booms. That is the only fact that is known. As to who did it and why, we can only surmise. Rumor has it that the man was not very large, that the yank he gave the rope was expressive of a jubilant frame of mind and was surprisingly vigorous. Some say that the suddenness and vigor of that pull betray inexperience, and point the finger of suspicion at those in high places. You say this is preposterous? You are right; it is preposterous. Why should a great man so far forget his dignity as to pull on a hempen bell rope, and in the dead of night? Surely petty victory cannot unbalance the great. They are the dupes of vain imaginings who . . . say that in Chapel the next morning whenever Prexy spoke, the whole place was pervaded with an atmosphere of guilt and also of repentance. They err in judgment who whisper about that it was in absent-minded self-reproach that he brought in that allusion, "How are the mighty fallen! Tell it not in Gath; publish it not in the streets of Askelon."

impressive: their loss to Muskingum in 1912 was their first in nine debates. Then for two years the team had a 1-1 record. So when in 1915 the debaters defeated both Pitt and Westminster, there was great joy on campus.

The literary societies were showing their age. Faculty members noted the decline and tried with little success to revive interest. The old pattern of declamation, essay, oration, and debate each week had demanded significant commitment from the students. Preparation now became more casual, partly because other extracurricular activities were competing for the time and energy of the students—dramatics, music, intercollegiate oratory and debate. The annual contests, however, continued to be high points of interest and emotion. Members came, wearing their pink or white carnations, to cheer their contestants, to wait anxiously for the decision of the judges, and to celebrate victory or suffer in defeat. The banquets given by each society to honor their participants in the contest were among the social highlights of the year.

The societies remained a significant part of campus life longer at Geneva than elsewhere, partly because Geneva chose not to allow fraternities and sororities. Reformed Presbyterians conscientiously believed that it was wrong to take an oath of secrecy before knowing what sorts of things were to be kept secret. The secrecy of fraternities and sororities was morally offensive to them. At Geneva it was the Aletheorians and Adelphics that provided the associations offered elsewhere by the Greek letter societies.

The college gradually exercised more oversight of the dormitory. It had originally been run almost independently—the college leased the building for a modest sum to a steward, who rented rooms to women students, provided board for men and women at a rate set by the college, and (it was hoped) created an attractive atmosphere for students. The effectiveness of this plan depended very much on the steward in charge. To integrate the dormitory more into the life of the college, Gyla MacDowell, who was appointed professor of English in

1907, was also named to the new office of Dean of Women. She was asked to live in the dormitory and to be responsible for its atmosphere and the behavior of its residents. She found that combined role very demanding and asked for an assistant dean who would be the head resident in the dormitory. For some years Helen McClintock, who taught French and German, filled this role well. Eventually she found it almost impossible to prepare for classes, answer the telephone, oversee the dining hall, and deal with student problems and discipline. The board then appointed as matron a woman who did not have faculty responsibilities.

Social life began each fall with the Thousand Mile Walk, sponsored by the YMCA and the YWCA, at which every fellow had the opportunity to meet every girl. At the end of the year came Commencement Week: the baccalaureate service, receptions by the literary societies, recitals, Class Day, and the graduation exercises as its climax. Through the year there were several traditional events: the Westerners' Picnic, for students from beyond the Mississippi;

Flag Rush. A traditional freshman-sophomore battle: the freshmen put the "flag" on a pole and defended it—could the sophomores get it down? In 1917, "the freshmen were declared winners by the judges at the end of thirty minutes' fighting, and scores of first-year classmen hailed the victory . . . , while Freshman lassies hastened to apply first aid to the many bruises their heroes had received in defense of the flag." (*The Cabinet*, Commencement Issue, 1917.) Photograph courtesy Marshall W. Smith.

Metheny reported to the trustees that he had provided "rigid training" in calisthenics for Geneva men. From the Downie Collection.

This 33rd Street field was the home for Geneva football until Reeves Field was opened in 1925. From the Downie Collection.

Halloween parties; the football banquet at which President George entertained the members of the football team and their guests; the literary society banquets for their contestants; and the spring festival, when the women students performed folk dances in honor of the Queen of the May.

President George was deeply committed to the developing of character in the students under his care. He was typical of the America of his time in seeing Christianity primarily in its role of producing character: men and women of honor and integrity, of perseverance, of courage, and of social concern. He was impatient with theology and uneasy with an evangelism that focused on conversion rather than on character. To produce character he saw disciplined study as more effective than visiting speakers. In a report to the Board of Trustees he wrote:

It is so much easier to listen to a talker saying good things than it is to get down and dig out Greek roots that the student welcomes talk. But he needs the discipline of digging.

Brainerd Metheny was photographed in his office in the Johnston Gymnasium. He served as athletic director and coach from 1913 to 1916. The Metheny Field House is named for him. Photograph courtesy Marshall W. Smith.

In significant measure, the college atmosphere came to reflect the president's definition of Christianity. The YMCA at Geneva lost its evangelistic purpose and announced its goal "to be primarily a Booster's Club in Geneva." Topics for meetings in the fall of 1912 included "College Spirit," "Courtesy in College," and "The Care of College Property." Even in this atmosphere, however, influential students were deeply involved in the Student Volunteer Movement, committing themselves to mission work at home and abroad; and numbers of men and women left Geneva with a commitment to Jesus Christ for service as ministers, as missionaries, and as earnest Christians in lay pursuits.

The 1910 basketball team, with Arthur McKean as coach, had a 7-2-1 record. Members of the team were John Patterson, captain, Brainerd Metheny, —— Miller, William Edwards, Brown Sterrett, Claude Nelson, Charles Stewart, and —— Littell. From the Downie Collection.

During the school year of 1915–16, President George communicated to the board his intention to resign at the end of the year. He did not enjoy administration, and he suggested that he had remained as president largely out of respect for his father, who had recently died. He planned to return to Harvard University for further graduate work. The board, recognizing his desire to return to research, reluctantly accepted his resignation. They insisted, despite his disclaimer, that he had been a capable administrator, and they noted gratefully his gentlemanly conduct, his studious habits, and his influence on Geneva students.

The "G" Men of 1914 posed for their photograph on the steps of Old Main. Photo courtesy Marshall W. Smith.

Geneva fans wait for the train to New Wilmington for the Westminster game. From the Downie Collection.

It will give President George sincere pleasure to have you and your company dine with him in honor of the Football Team of 1913 at the Dormitory, Thursday Evening, December fourth, at 7 o'clock.

R. S. V. P.

President George entertained the football team and their "company" at a banquet at the end of the season. The invitations were handwritten, this one probably to George Fee. From the Downie Collection.

Above: The women's basketball team, about 1916. Photograph courtesy Marshall W. Smith.

Below: This race is being run during a dual meet with Allegheny College, 1916. Photograph courtesy Marshall W. Smith.

This Shakespearean scene, performed by the seniors in 1916 for their class play, is in honor of the tercentenary of Shakespeare's death in 1616. From the Downie Collection.

In 1916, the Oratorical Department, under the direction of Mrs. Carothers McConagha, presented George Bernard Shaw's *Arms and the Man*. From the Downie Collection.

Skating on the Beaver River was a highly popular winter sport—"the better the ice, the worse the grades."

Soon after the college moved to Beaver Falls a street railway was established, its horse cars bringing students as far as the foot of the hill where the stables were located. Later the line was extended and electrified. This photograph pictures a street car rounding the corner of College Avenue and Thirty-second Street. A common student prank was greasing the rails at the corner so the cars could not get up the hill. Photograph courtesy Marshall W. Smith.

In the original deed from the Harmony Society the college was given the right to build a boathouse along the river. There is no record that the right was used, but a lot of canoeing was done anyway!

Ada Wilson (Hutcheson), Queen of the
May in 1916, knights one of her subjects.

This is a portrait of the 1913 May Queen.

Above: Intercollegiate debate was a highly competitive sport at Geneva during the George administration. Here Geneva fans wait at the station to welcome home the debate team after victories over Muskingum and Westminster. "The Triumphant Parade." From the Downie Collection.

Below: Geneva women danced the Maypole dance in honor of the queen.

FIVE

THE CURRICULUM REVOLUTION
1916—1923

*G*eneva responded cautiously to the ferment in the eastern universities.

The board found an obvious successor to President George in Renwick H. Martin. Martin was a graduate of Geneva, Class of 1895, and of the Reformed Presbyterian Theological Seminary. In 1899 he had become the first pastor of the College Hill Reformed Presbyterian congregation, where a number of the college faculty worshiped. In his seventeen years of service there, he had become well-known in Beaver County. He was chosen to the Board of Trustees in 1907 and at once elected as its secretary. He had even moonlighted as director of physical education for one enjoyable but hectic year. Both for him and for the college, the transition was easy. He had been close to President George, and as president he pursued the same academic goals.

The gradual changes in the curriculum under George came to a focus in Martin's first year, culminating in the largest single curricular change in Geneva's history. That 1917 change was significant both in philosophy and in structure. In the 1870s, Harvard's President Eliot had challenged the traditional view that there was a core of

knowledge that marked the educated person and therefore a single curriculum. Eliot believed that students had varied gifts and interests and differing professional goals, and that they should be encouraged to develop their individual gifts and pursue their personal goals. He therefore opened a greatly broadened curriculum to the free "election" of the student. There were no required courses at Harvard. Harvard's model was copied by some colleges and vigorously opposed by others. The traditional curriculum was in disarray.

As colleges searched for some coherence in the midst of this disarray, an emerging consensus was to create a number of "majors" from which students might choose, each major consisting of courses in a single area of knowledge.

President Renwick Harper Martin Renwick Harper Martin (1872–1958) was president of Geneva from 1916 to 1920. After his presidency he served for many years on the staff of the National Reform Association, especially concerned with issues of temperance and Sabbath observance.

Students took a prescribed number of courses within a major to provide a focus for their study; they broadened their education by a required distribution across the curriculum; the rest of their courses they could elect as they chose.

Geneva responded cautiously to the ferment in the eastern universities. By introducing the B.S. in the 1870s and strengthening it in the 1890s, by introducing the Latin-Scientific course in 1908, and by broadening the number of courses available, Geneva had responded to students' changing needs and desires. By moving slowly, it avoided some of the curricular disarray of the times. Then in 1917, Geneva introduced a completely new curricular structure, consisting of nine majors. Six of the majors led to the B.A. degree: Greek; Latin and Greek; modern languages; philosophy and education; English; and history. Three majors led to the B.S. degree: chemistry, mathematics, and biology. This curricular change was accompanied by a new academic calendar and school day. Two semesters replaced three terms; and classes were extended from forty-five minutes to an hour.

During World War I, President Emeritus W. P. Johnston stands with his son, Archie, who was chosen president in 1920. From the Downie Collection.

In 1914 the Armstrong Cork Company began the production of fire brick in their plant at the foot of College Hill. The process involved mixing ground cork with the clay before it was fired. As the cork burned out in the firing, the brick became porous, to be used for lining furnaces in steel mills. For some decades, therefore, the aroma of burnt cork was part of the Geneva experience. That and other features of College Hill life are captured in this bit of verse from *The Cabinet* in November 1917:

Welcome to our midst, ye Freshmen,

Welcome to these halls of fame;

Welcome to the fields and campus,

To the sunshine and the rain.

Welcome to the fog and cork dust,

Welcome to the dirt and smoke;

Welcome to the noise of engines,

And the feeling, "I'm dead broke."

Note the contrast with the pastoral location of the college when it first moved to Beaver Falls in 1880.

In its new structure, Geneva kept its commitment to two curricular principles. The first maintained that there was a core of knowledge to which a college education should introduce all its students, though the content of that core was changing. Language remained part of the core, now including modern languages. Courses in language were required for entrance and at least one year of college language for graduation. Some high school Latin was still required for the B.A. Mathematics remained, probably more for its importance in contemporary science than for its historic role in the curriculum. Acquaintance with Western culture was acquired by reading history in English rather than the classics in Greek or Latin. Courses in English and public speaking trained college students in communication. The second curricular principle held that there were courses distinctive to Geneva's character that must be required of all students. At the heart of the curriculum were the courses in Bible, which was in Geneva's view the infallible guide for faith and life. The courses in political science continued the commitment to the relevance of Jesus Christ to political life. The Board of Corporators, usually wary of change, took the new curriculum in stride, praising "the adaptation of the College

Course to the necessities of those who desire to prepare themselves for the duties of life."

As these curricular changes were being put into effect, the United States entered World War I on April 6, 1917. At the meeting of the Board of Trustees a week later, "the president of the college was authorized to offer to the President of the United States the buildings and grounds of the college for any use which the government might desire. . . ." President Martin asked: "What can Geneva do?" It did a lot. Martin later remarked, "The war spirit dominates our college life."

In fact, since its outbreak in Europe in 1914, the war had increasingly dominated the college atmosphere. In some ways, the students had entered the war before their country did. The pages of *The Cabinet* were full of attacks on the Kaiser. The February 1917 issue ran an editorial entitled, "We Are Not Neutral," and quoted the famous Lowell poem:

> *Once to every man and nation*
> *Comes the moment to decide,*
> *In the strife of truth with falsehood,*
> *For the good or evil side.*

With the formal entrance of the United States into the war, the campus changed. There were emotional scenes as students went off to camp. Faculty members left for the army or other war service. Biology professor Walter Marshall, physical education director Brainerd Metheny, and the registrar Earl Moore were drafted. Faculty members A. A. Johnston, Sloane Martin, and Harry Wylie volunteered in various capacities. Evangeline Metheny, who taught English, joined the Red Cross for service in Palestine. Women from the community took over the YMCA room for Red Cross activities. There were weekly briefings in chapel on the news from the front. The college began offering special "war" courses: the history of the war; courses in physiology, hygiene, and food conservation; and a study of Christian internationalism taught by the president. Even the usual May Day performance broke with tradition, for it was transformed into a patriotic festival. Women costumed as Columbia and the states replaced the May Queen and her court. The Maypole dancers wound red, white, and blue

The Student Army Training Corps drills on the Geneva field at 33rd Street, 1918.

The first graduate of Geneva killed in World War I was Dean Buchanan of the Class of 1916. After his graduation, he had served as a missionary in Persia before enlisting in the army. From the Downie Collection. Another alumnus killed was John Lincoln Downie, for whom the Downie oratorical prize is named.

streamers instead of the time-honored gold and white.

The most visible participation of the college in activities related to the war was in hosting a unit of the Student Army Training Corps. The third floor of Old Main was turned into a barracks, including the rooms of the literary societies, which ceased operation for the time. The ninety-five members of the Corps arrived, with scant warning, in September, 1918—shortly before the Armistice in November, as it turned out—and left before the end of the semester. Martin met willingly the inevitable complications for the college; but he was greatly distressed by the attitude of the first officer, who had no sympathy with the standards of the college and who did what he could to challenge them. Martin was eventually able to have him replaced and gratefully found his successor a very different sort of officer. In the end, Martin reported to the Board of Trustees:

The presence of the SATC during the first part of the [college] year gave rise to many difficulties which taxed the administration to the utmost. Out of it all Geneva has come, preserved and guided by the One who never slumbers nor sleeps. Geneva still stands as she has always stood, faithful to Christ and loyal to our country.

When former president W. H. George enlisted in the Ambulance Corps for service overseas, the Geneva women knit a blanket for him, gold, with the "G" in white. Photograph from the Downie Collection.

Geneva Glee Club 1916-7.

Chalfant & Boylin.

One hundred sixty-four Geneva students and alumni served in the armed services during the war. Five died: Hall Braham, Dean Buchanan, Forbes Downie, John Downie, and Norman McCreary. Professor Marshall of the faculty died of pneumonia while he was in training camp.

The Reformed Presbyterian Church honored the members of the denomination who served in the war, and especially those who lost their lives, by endowing at Geneva the Memorial Bible Chair, "to the end that the first phrase of our college motto be emphasized as the second has been, that *Pro Christo et Patria* may shine forth with a new meaning at this dawn of a new day. . . ." With the creation of the chair in Bible there was for the first time a faculty member who could give all his time to Bible courses. In 1920, John Coleman was chosen as the first occupant of the chair. He and his wife, Mary Willson Coleman, revised the required course in Bible to make it a thorough coverage of Bible history. He also created a number of elective courses, enough that a student could major in Bible. When in

1921 he assumed the added responsibility of the required course in political science, his wife and other faculty members shared the Bible courses. In 1926, J. Boyd Tweed joined the Bible department. Both Coleman and Tweed were men of high Christian character, and they were compelling teachers. Because they both taught required courses they had unusual opportunity to touch the lives of Geneva students.

During and after World War I, Geneva's enrollment rose rapidly. It had peaked earlier in 1908–09 at 165, but early in the next decade leveled off at just over 125 students. Then by 1918, the enrollment had doubled. This welcome increase in students strained the physical resources of the campus; the number of resident women overflowed the capacity of the dormitory. There was talk of enlarging the building; but Robert Clarke as usual saw beyond the immediate needs. With a substantial contribution from Mary Elizabeth Gregg McKee, whose father had been a college trustee, he was able to move toward the construction of a new

The men's glee club began informally about 1910 with a group of men who liked to sing. Professor Wylie organized and trained them. By the middle of the decade they were making an annual tour to publicize the college. This picture is of the 1916–1917 club.

As the enrollment of Geneva grew after World War I, the 1888 dormitory could no longer accommodate the resident women. In 1921 a new women's dormitory was opened, named McKee Hall for Mary Elizabeth Gregg McKee, whose generosity made it possible. Mrs. McKee was the wife of David McKee, a Reformed Presbyterian pastor in Clarinda, Iowa, and the daughter of David Gregg, a trustee of the college in the nineteenth century.

women's dormitory. To locate the building appropriately, the trustees secured part of the McCartney property adjoining the campus; and the McCartney house, Ferncliffe, was moved some rods north to its present location. McKee Hall was designed by William Eckles and completed for occupancy in 1921. It was a handsome addition to the campus, providing more attractive and comfortable quarters for resident women. The old dormitory, renamed North Hall, was used to house men for another generation.

In President Martin's report to the board at the end of his first year, he said, "Our students are moral; most are also

religious. One of the things we most desire is the deepening of the religious life at Geneva." This suggests a shift in his emphasis as president from "character," which had been so important to his predecessor, to "faith." He believed the best way to accomplish a deeper religious life was to invite "speakers . . . who by words and life could encourage faith among the students." The dislocations of World War I occupied his attention enough that he did not develop this program very extensively during his short presidency. There are records of visiting speakers who encouraged volunteering for foreign mission work. In 1920, he arranged for "special services," addressed by two

Reformed Presbyterian ministers; and he noted with appreciation that seventy-five students had signed cards indicating a commitment to Jesus Christ and His service. The YMCA and the YWCA continued their meetings during his presidency, and Geneva students continued to participate actively in state and national conferences.

Geneva's athletic program was becoming more organized. In 1912, the physical director was also named the coach for the college teams. The first occupant of the post found it difficult to be responsible for both the physical training classes and for coaching. But from 1913 through 1916, the position was held by Brainerd Metheny, who was able to combine the two roles. He reported to the Board of Trustees that "rigid training" had been "well adhered to" in the gym classes; and during his four years he had three winning football seasons and two winning basketball seasons. The track team was doing well; and in 1915, the tennis team defeated Carnegie Tech, Grove City, and Westminster.

A women's glee club, pictured here, was organized in 1918–19. For the next two years there was a mixed chorus; then a men's glee club alone until 1925 when a women's glee club was reorganized. The new club had an active life, including an annual engagement in Atlantic City each spring. In 1938 the two glee clubs were again joined as The Genevans.

There was an active program for women's physical education, headed after 1916 by Edna George, who also served as librarian. She had been a member of the basketball team that had two undefeated seasons, 6-0 in 1909 (154-31 points) and 10-0 (186–62 points) in 1910. During her long tenure at Geneva she played a major role in the life of Geneva women. The women were barred from the gym during football season, and for their recreation Miss George took them on long walks—an attractive option during Pennsylvania's beautiful autumns. During the winter they had a physical education program in the gym with regular Swedish and German exercises. In the spring, the

women prepared their program of folk dances for the May Day festivities. Intercollegiate basketball games with such schools as Pitt, Allegheny, and Westminster created an exciting activity for the women who participated. For both men and women, athletics were a major part of their Geneva life. Not only were there the varsity teams (taking up "some of our time, three-fourths of our conversation, and all our lung power," said *The Cabinet*, which covered athletics in detail), but there were scrub teams with their own schedules and lots of intramural games, especially between class teams.

World War I did not seriously affect the athletic program at Geneva. In the spring of 1917, as the country entered the war, the track season was replaced by military drill for the men, three afternoons a week, led by one of the trustees, C. R. May. Otherwise the sports programs continued. When Metheny was drafted into the army, Philip Bridenbaugh was chosen to replace him and served until 1922. In his five years at Geneva Bridenbaugh had four winning football seasons. It was he who held the first football camp, in 1919, at Camp Geneva on the Little Beaver Creek, with ten days of hard practice and good food. In his first year, the basketball team had a 13-2 record, followed by two more winning seasons, especially notable because Geneva scheduled such teams as Yale, Princeton, Pitt, and West Virginia.

In the summer of 1920, President Martin presented his resignation to the Board of Trustees, pleading weariness with the responsibilities of the position. Archibald Johnston, who was teaching history and economics, agreed to serve as Acting President during the presidential search; at the end of the year he was unanimously elected president. The son of William Pollock Johnston, he was the fourth Johnston president of the college. A graduate of Geneva and of the Reformed Presbyterian Seminary, he also held degrees from Princeton University and Princeton Seminary. Before joining the Geneva faculty in 1916, he had been the pastor of the Reformed Presbyterian congregation in Walton, New York.

As president he was committed to the academic course set by Presidents George and Martin. He actively pursued

After the death of R. M. Downie, Class of 1881, Geneva alumni provided funds to purchase his house across College Avenue in 1926. It was named Alumni Hall and has since been the home of the Music Department.

the accreditation of the college by what was then called The Association of Colleges and Preparatory Schools of the Middle States and Maryland. The most tangible remaining barrier was Geneva's sparse endowment, which stood at a slender half of the Association's requirement of $500,000. Happily for Geneva, the Association was willing to accept as an alternative the denomination's annual contribution, then set at $20,000, which would be the five percent income on a $400,000 endowment. To reassure the accreditors, the trustees personally guaranteed Synod's contribution. In December 1922, Geneva received word of her accreditation by the Middle States Association.

The formal entrance to Old Main is from the south, but for many years most people used this College Avenue entrance. At one point there were fish ponds on either side of the walk. The lamps were the gift of the Class of 1913.

The academic program continued to expand. Most of the new majors established in 1916 had broadened their offerings since then: biology courses, for instance, had risen from seven to fifteen; in English and history seven courses had grown to twelve. A major in Bible was established. More choices were available, and more advanced work was offered within the majors.

The curriculum also expanded to meet vocational needs in the community. In 1920, Geneva established a Department of Engineering, beginning with a two-year course leading either to a surveying job or to transfer to an engineering school. The trustees explained in their report to the 1921 Synod that "Geneva is located in the heart of a great manufacturing center and therefore has a special opportunity to meet the peculiar demands of such a community." Teacher training was a continuing need, because the Pennsylvania legislature was continuing to raise the qualifications for teachers. To have a permanent certificate, teachers were now needing the equivalent of two years of college courses. This rise in certification requirements taxed

the capacity of existing teachers' colleges. Rather than open a new school in the Beaver County area to provide such courses, the State Department of Public Instruction in 1920 approved the Geneva program, which H. H. Wylie had earlier designed to meet the state requirements. In 1924, Geneva created the degree of Bachelor of Science in Education for students who met state requirements for certification along with Geneva's requirements for a degree.

The summer school and extension programs, begun for teacher training, were broadened to offer a wide variety of college classes. Demand for such courses steadily increased, as Wylie noted in his description of the Extension School in the 1921 *Genevan*, attracting a variety of people with differing motivations, "day laborers, office workers, school supervisors, Sunday School workers, clerks, librarians, housewives." In the Class of 1922 were eleven graduates who had taken *all* their college work "in extension," a pattern followed by many students who made their way evening after evening, year after year, to a Geneva diploma. This was especially

true after World War II. In 1957, more than twelve hundred students were taking advantage of this road to a Geneva degree.

Enrollment in the traditional program also grew very rapidly during this period, reflecting an increasing nationwide desire for a college education. By the school year 1921–22, the enrollment in day school was 504, four times as many as in 1915. The faculty grew to meet the demands of a larger student body and the larger curriculum. The college building, awkwardly large for one hundred students in 1881, now had to be carefully scheduled to provide rooms for classes. Some additional space was provided in 1926 when the college acquired the house of R. M. Downie across College Avenue. It was named Alumni Hall in recognition of alumni contributions toward its cost. It became the home of the Music Department, which had long needed more space and more privacy. No longer did aspiring musicians practicing their scales distract classes in Greek and Shakespeare. The physical move of the department was the occasion for changing its status from an auxiliary enterprise and making it a regular part of the college and of the curriculum. (Acquiring the Downie house was the first extension of the campus across College Avenue; one unintended consequence was the creation of a new extracurricular course in pedestrian survival, not officially part of the Geneva core but a necessary part of the curriculum!)

College life, which had been somewhat interrupted by World War I, blossomed again. The inter-society contests were revived in 1920 when a generous alumnus provided a silver loving cup to be presented to the society that was victorious three times. In the fifth year the Aletheorians won their third victory and kept the trophy. Lively intercollegiate competition in oratory and debate continued during the 1920s. By 1928 the debate team, coached by Robert Clarke, had won forty of their last forty-nine debates. In 1929, John Dodds, Geneva's intercollegiate orator, won the Pennsylvania state title.

Professor Gyla McDowell, always concerned for culture, organized a lyceum program, bringing to Geneva such artists as the soprano Madame Schumann-Heink, the pianist Olga Samaroff, the poet Edwin Markham, and Tony Sarg with his marionettes. In dedicating the 1922 *Genevan* to Miss McDowell, the editors wrote: "Her joy has ever been to bring to those with whom she comes in contact a wider appreciation of life." She was one of several influential women on the faculty in the 1920s. Beulah Wilson, back from missionary service in Cuba, taught Spanish. Isabelle Stewart created a French "circle" on campus, in addition to organizing a student club named *Le Cercle Français*. Mrs. H. H. Wylie first taught as a substitute for her husband

Geneva has had since 1880 a governing structure once common but by 1920 unusual. The Board of Corporators is elected by the Synod and Presbyteries of the Reformed Presbyterian Church to hold title to the college and have the final control of major decisions. The Corporators elect the Board of Trustees as the operating board. Typically it has been through the Board of Corporators rather than directly to the trustees that the denomination expresses its aspirations and concerns for the college.

during his study leave, then continued to teach as his responsibilities broadened. After his death in 1923 she returned to the University of Chicago to earn the Ph.D. degree, then taught psychology and chaired the department. M. Carothers McConagha and Edith Schillinger established strong traditions in dramatics and oratory.

As the college grew more sophisticated—and therefore more expensive to operate—Johnston recognized that the Reformed Presbyterian Church did not itself have the resources to support an accredited institution. He also knew that if the college failed to maintain its quality and standing, it would serve neither Reformed Presbyterian students nor others well. Geneva needed support from beyond the denomination, not only from the wider pool of students who might come for the education it offered, but also from the financial generosity of the local community.

One graceful way to encourage support was to provide the community with more participation in college governance. Since 1855, successive college charters had required that the trustees be members of the Reformed Presbyterian Church. For some years, it is true, there had been "consultative" members of the Board of Trustees, representing alumni and the community, some of them deeply involved with the work of the board. But they had no vote. Johnston therefore proposed to amend the college charter by

adding nine members to the twelve-member board. Three would be women chosen from the Reformed Presbyterian Church; three would be chosen from the alumni; and three would be community businessmen. Denominational control would be safeguarded: the fifteen Reformed Presbyterians would constitute a majority of the board; and all trustees would be elected, as before, by the Board of Corporators, all of whom were members of the Reformed Presbyterian Church.

In proposing changes in the membership of the Board of Trustees, Johnston was not intending to change the Christian character of the college. He stated his position to the trustees in the spring of 1921:

In the direction of an education which is adequately Christian lies the path of duty and success. Perhaps, the small college would have little reason for existence were it not that there is realized the necessity to teach the vital truths of our Christian faith, the inspiration of the Bible, the fact of the incarnation, the need of the atonement, the place of Christ in the political, as well as the ecclesiastical sphere. More and more, Geneva should be known as a Christian college in teaching and in life.
But in that statement he made only an oblique reference to the college's ties to the denomination, speaking of "the place of Christ in the political . . . sphere."

The Board of Trustees was divided in its response to the proposal. Several

members were strongly opposed to the change, fearing dilution of denominational control. Their fear had deep roots: seventy years earlier a similar concern had led to the inclusion in the 1855 charter of a vigorous statement that the college "shall be and remain forever under the direction of persons known and acknowledged members of the Reformed Presbyterian Church." Their fear also had a current relevance. In this period, well-known colleges were ending denominational control, partly for greater freedom, but also in the hope of broader financial support. John D. Rockefeller and Andrew Carnegie had created foundations to aid the cause of higher education, and both foundations had denied grants to church-controlled colleges, in part because presumably such schools had the resources of their denominations behind them. Such respected colleges as Bowdoin, Wesleyan, Hanover, and Occidental cut denominational ties. Denominational control of colleges was thus a significant issue of the time. In the Reformed Presbyterian Church, in fact, there was some sentiment for more denomination-

al influence over Geneva rather than less. The editor of the *Christian Nation*, the church paper, argued that Geneva should be a "Covenanter college for Covenanter youth. . . . Our first aim is not to build a great college, but to teach our young people the distinctive principles of the Covenanter church."

Faced with a board divided over a proposal he considered crucial to the future of Geneva and with division in the denomination, Johnston resigned during the 1922–23 school year. He was joined in his resignation by three influential members of the faculty, Robert Colwell and Professor and Mrs. Wylie. Tension was very high.

When the proposal came to a vote in the Board of Trustees, the majority of the board approved the proposed change in the charter, which was then approved by the Board of Corporators and, after intense discussion, by Synod. With the change approved, the Wylies withdrew their resignations and Colwell asked for a leave of absence; but Johnston persisted in his decision.

During the summer of 1923 the Board of Corporators held the first

election of trustees under the amended charter. Since the college moved to Pennsylvania in 1880 trustees had been elected for one-year terms. Usually they had been reelected until they died or resigned, but legally the whole board was up for election each year. In this case, only four of the twelve previous members were reelected, an unprecedented turnover. Eight were replaced, including those who had opposed the new charter. The nine newly created positions were filled as specified: three women from the Reformed Presbyterian Church, three local businessmen, and three alumni. The women chosen were welcomed on the board and were assigned responsibilities. Despite changes in the membership of the board, there was continuity: R. M. Young was reelected president of the board; and some of the businessmen and alumni elected had already been playing active roles in the life of the board as consultative members.

SIX

THE FIRST PEARCE YEARS
1923 — 1940

The immediate task of the new board was to find a successor for President Johnston.

To that position it elected McLeod Milligan Pearce of the Geneva Class of 1896. He had served Reformed Presbyterian pastorates in St. Louis, Pittsburgh, and Philadelphia, and when he was chosen president he was an editor with the American Sunday School Union. Pearce had close ties with the college: his father, William Pearce, had played a major part in the construction of Old Main, and his brother, Robert M. Pearce, had been a valued member of the Board of Trustees until his early death. When Pearce became president, the college purchased the McCartney house, Ferncliffe, for his residence. Although Pearce's term as president began in an atmosphere of tension, it became the longest in Geneva's history, lasting a quarter of a century. After his first year in office, Synod's committee on college affairs commended the trustees for their choice:

He brought to his task a manly piety based on a keen sense of justice and obligation to deal fairly and squarely with the various constituencies of the college.

"The Athlete." This sketch of a football player, drawn by John Steuart Curry for the 1920 *Genevan*, symbolizes the importance of football in Geneva life during the 1920s.

President Mcleod Milligan Pearce McLeod Milligan Pearce (1874–1948) was president of Geneva from 1923 to 1948, the longest presidency in Geneva's 150-year history.

During the 1920 season what seems to have been the first Geneva homecoming occurred. The returning alumni joined the students in celebrating Geneva's 20-0 victory over Allegheny with a rally in the chapel and a bonfire in the evening.

Football dominated the 1920s at Geneva. There were winning seasons in 1920 and 1921 under Coach Philip Bridenbaugh, in 1923 under Coach Tom Davies, and in 1925 under the legendary Bo McMillin.

Excitement climaxed on October 2, 1926, when McMillin and the Geneva football team journeyed to Cambridge, Massachusetts, and defeated Harvard University, then a proud football power, 16-7, in its season opener—the first time Harvard had lost an opening game! During the rest of the fall, Geneva held Cornell to a one-touchdown victory, lost narrowly to Grove City, won the rest of its games, then defeated Oglethorpe in a post-season game in Jacksonville, Florida. The next year the team was undefeated, a season marred only by a 0-0 tie with Bucknell. On that team was

Cal Hubbard, the most famous Geneva athlete, named to several All-American teams and the only person in both the Football Hall of Fame (as a tackle) and the Baseball Hall of Fame (as an umpire). In 1924–25, the area colleges, with Geneva as a leader, organized the Tri-State Conference. Geneva was co-champion with Thiel the first year, then conference champion for the next three years.

The physical symbol of football's importance was the construction of Reeves Field. The familiar old field on 33rd Street would no longer hold the crowds coming to see Geneva play. To provide a new stadium the Reeves family donated land south of the campus along College Avenue in memory of John Reeves, Sr., who as agent of the Harmony Society had presented the college with its original ten-acre campus. The hillside took some grading, surely; but when graded it was an impressive spot for a stadium, the six thousand seats looking out over the field to the hills beyond the river. It was dedicated in the fall of 1925, when Geneva played Westminster—and won.

Basketball was consistently strong. Under coaches Paul Cutwright, Bo McMillin, and Kenneth Loeffler, the team had winning seasons from 1924 to 1936, except for 1926–27. For seven of those seasons, from 1928 to 1935, Loeffler was the coach, compiling an impressive 93-53 record.

Geneva made headlines in the *New York Times* of October 3, 1926, by defeating Harvard in its opening game 16-7.

The New York Times front page, Sunday, October 3, 1926 — Sports Section 10, featuring headlines "63,000 SEE YANKEES BEAT CARDINALS, 2-1; PENNOCK'S TRIUMPH" and "HARVARD HUMBLED BY GENEVA, 16."

Justice Robert Wagner Tossing Out the First Ball at the Stadium Yesterday. With the Democratic Nominee for U. S. Senator Are Mayor Walker and Colonel Jacob Ruppert, Owner of the Yankees (extreme right).

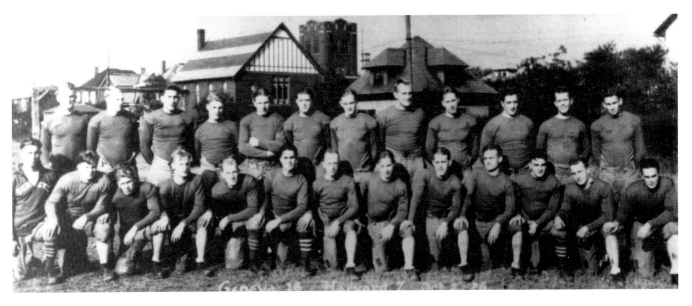

The 1926 football team is the most famous in Geneva's history, especially for its victory over Harvard. The 1927 *Genevan*.

As Geneva's football success increased the number of spectators, the 33rd Street field was no longer adequate. The Reeves family gave Geneva land along College Avenue below the college for a stadium. It opened for the football season of 1925, Geneva playing Westminster for the opening game.

Bo McMillin coached football at Geneva from 1925 to 1927, the legendary years.

Geneva had an outstanding record in track. For the first ten years of the Tri-State Conference, Geneva took the championship. Professor Robert Park was a beloved and effective coach, attracting talented track men, among them two notable runners, Bill Butler (who broke the Geneva record in every event he entered) and Howard Spencer. The relay team regularly ranked near the top in the Penn Relays. In 1925, cross-country and tennis became intercollegiate sports, introduced by Athletic Director A. C. Edgecombe. From 1929 to 1933, the Geneva cross-country team took three district championships. The Geneva tennis team was a power in the Tri-State Conference, with three championship seasons and two years in second place. The 1933 *Genevan* proudly noted that the team was ranked eleventh nationally by the U. S. Lawn Tennis Association.

Women's basketball continued in the 1920s to be an intercollegiate sport. Geneva women, coached by Edna George, played such area colleges as Beaver, Westminster, Thiel, and Carnegie Tech, with consistently winning seasons.

The Geneva relay team for 1930 consisted of Arthur Thomas, John Nave, Robert Nulton, and Dwight Piper. They were Tri-State Conference champions and placed second in the Penn Relay Carnival. The track team, coached by Professor Robert Park, dominated the Tri-State Conference for a decade from the organization of the conference until 1935.

In the spring of 1926, with Professor Isabelle Stewart making the arrangements, the basketball team took an eastern trip, playing Dickinson College and New York University. Intercollegiate competition was dropped in 1927, but George and her successors continued a vigorous program of athletics for women on the campus. Women were given points for a variety of athletic activities and were awarded a coveted "G" when they had accumulated five hundred points. There was an active women's intramural program in badminton, volleyball, and basketball. The top basketball players organized two teams—"Yale" and "Princeton"—and the Yale-Princeton game, with its intense rivalry, faculty

Bill Butler, Class of 1928, was one of Geneva's most noted track stars. During his time at Geneva he broke the college record in every category he entered. The 1928 *Genevan*.

cheerleaders, and a crowded Johnston Gym was one of the highlights of the college year. There were occasional intercollegiate games arranged informally; but it was not until the mid-1970s that Title IX stimulated the revival of intercollegiate sports for women.

There was a disturbing side to athletics as well. At Geneva, as on the national scene, football's appetite for money and power seemed almost impossible to control. How could Geneva keep football non-professional, when competition for players was so intense? How could Geneva keep football in some reasonable relationship to the rest of the college? How could Geneva remain committed to the Christian faith and life in the face of intense pressures to compromise for the sake of athletic success? Though Geneva claimed to stand for "clean" athletics, an audit of the books in 1923—insisted on by the trustees—

showed that some of the college bills of outstanding athletes were either left unpaid or quietly written off. The board reacted to that information by adopting a strong statement of policy:

That none of the resources of Geneva College, including money received from gate receipts at athletic contests, guarantees from other colleges for games, gifts to the college for athletic purposes . . . be used in any way whatsoever to provide remuneration of any kind to students who represent the college on athletic teams.

The board appointed a committee to formulate a plan to administer the policy. But so absolute a policy proved impossible to implement, and the issue remained.

The drive for winning teams skewed the priorities of the college in other ways. Over the protest of several trustees, the board approved paying the football coach $3,000 for the 1923 season, more than senior faculty members were receiving for a year's teaching. In 1925 the famous Bo McMillin was attracted to Geneva by a salary of $7,500, nearly double the salary of the president. Contributions for Reeves Field came easily, although the

Above: From her appointment in 1916 until 1932, when illness forced her to retire, Edna George was responsible for women's athletics. She coached the women's basketball team, created an outstanding program of intramurals for women, and directed the May Day celebration each spring. The 1921 *Genevan*.

Left: President Pearce stands with two outstanding science teachers at Geneva, William Cleland in physics and mathematics and Philip Coon in chemistry.

Theodore McMillion was an admired and effective teacher of biology at Geneva from 1926 until his retirement in 1974. The premedical program over which he presided was notable for its success in preparing students to enter medical school.

construction of the existing college buildings at Geneva had required a difficult search for funds. In the following years, the excesses of the middle 1920s were brought under control; but the problems in achieving what was then called "clean" athletics recurred in trustee discussions at least until World War II.

Dr. Pearce was the first president who did not teach, a reminder of the growing administrative responsibilities of a college president. And he presided over an expanding administrative structure. The office of Dean had been created in 1920 under President A. A. Johnston. Physics professor R. C. Colwell was appointed to the position, with the somewhat alarming job description that he was to perform "duties to be determined by the president." As the position developed, these duties were chiefly to deal with students in trouble over class attendance and scholastic standing. In that role one of Colwell's innovations was to institute a mid-semester examination, so that students could know how they were doing before

the end of the term. It was a sign of changing times that he expressed concern about pressures on the new breed of students working their way through college, often by jobs in the local factories. When Colwell left Geneva in 1925, Charles M. Lee succeeded him as dean.

In 1919, E. May Girvan was appointed "local treasurer." The responsibilities of the on-campus treasurer had for many years been assigned to a faculty member, then to other officials as a part of their duties. Miss Girvan was the first person to give her whole attention to the job—collecting tuition from students, paying salaries and other bills, superintending the operation of the dining hall and the bookstore. She held the post for over forty years until her retirement in 1960, although by that time her duties were shared by a number of others.

In 1922, Lulu McKinney was appointed the first full-time registrar. As the curriculum became more complex, the job of the registrar became both more complicated and more essential. She served both students and the college well by the meticulous records she kept. Like

Miss Girvan she spent the rest of her career at Geneva, retiring in 1952.

Robert Clarke continued his services to the college in fundraising, as assistant to the president. In 1924, James S. Martin joined the college staff, originally to continue the financial campaign begun the year before. As that campaign came to a close, he was named executive secretary, a title that covered such varied responsibilities as being purchasing agent for the college, supervising student publications, and organizing alumni activities. He was the first editor of the *Geneva Alumnus*, which began publication in 1924. This administrative structure continued with little change until late in Pearce's long presidency.

The Great Depression had a disastrous effect on the national economy and on the lives of many families, but it had surprisingly little impact on the operation of the college. At the depth of the depression, Geneva had its highest enrollment up to that point: 613 students were enrolled in the day school in 1932–33. (About six hundred other students were taking summer or extension classes.) In the following years, the day school enrollment decreased somewhat, but was only briefly below five hundred, a figure considered optimum at the beginning of the decade. One explanation for this stable enrollment despite the depression may have been that students from the community who now could not afford to go away to college enrolled in Geneva.

The income of the college did of course diminish. Income from investments declined; contributions from the denomination were down 50 percent by 1934. As Pearce noted sympathetically, some students were unable to keep their tuition paid, and for the two years 1932 to 1934 tuition income was down by about 25 percent. The lowered income was matched by lower expenditures. In fact the operating budget dropped from just over $300,000 in 1930–31 to just over $200,000 in 1933–1934. The staff was not cut, though during the winter of 1931 the trustees discussed the possibility. But beginning with the 1932–33 school year, faculty salaries were reduced. (Technically salaries were not changed, but faculty members were asked to "refund" 10 percent—and later 5 percent more—of their salaries by a deduction from their monthly pay checks. Half of the amount refunded was placed in a fund for student loans.) Survival, both for the college and for the faculty, was made possible by a drop in the Consumer Price Index by about 23 percent from 1929 to 1933. This eased the financial burden for faculty members and made almost automatic a significant reduction in the college operating budget.

The college maintained a stable course under the leadership of President Pearce. The board trusted him. It met only twice a year, except for an occasional called meeting, and the meetings were brief. There was little discussion of academic policy, or indeed of the general direction of the college.

Isabelle Stewart, beloved professor of French, had a contagious enthusiasm for French culture.

A chemistry laboratory looked like this about the year 1930.

McCartney Library was designed by William G. Eckles, who had earlier designed Johnston Gymnasium and McKee Hall.

Athletics continued to do well. Coach Loeffler's success in basketball continued for the first half of the 1930s, with Cliff Aultman as an outstanding member of the team. Coaches Howard Harpster, Jimmy Robertson, and Dirk Beede compiled a fine football record, 43-19-5 from 1930 to 1936, more than once bringing the conference championship to College Hill. The track team dominated the conference from its beginning in 1925 through 1935. Under the leadership of William Davies and Edna George, a more extensive program of intramural sports for men and women was developed, with 90 percent of the students participating.

The appearance of the campus changed greatly in the 1930s with the erection of McCartney Library. This elegant building, designed by William G. Eckles, has for more than six decades symbolized the centrality of books in a college education. Funds for the library were generously provided by the Misses Deal from Philadelphia, in honor of

Clarence E. Macartney, their former pastor at the Arch Street Presbyterian Church. Macartney had grown up beside the campus (his father was closely associated with Geneva from its revival after the Civil War until his death as professor emeritus in 1911). Macartney later served as pastor of the historic First Presbyterian Church in Pittsburgh. He was a lifelong friend of Geneva, and in his retirement returned to his childhood home in Ferncliffe, where he died in 1957. (He chose to spell his name differently, but asked that the library be named for his family and that it keep the family spelling of the name, McCartney.)

The magnificent stained glass throughout the building was created by Henry Lee Willet. The great window in the east reading room, depicting John Bunyan's *Pilgrim's Progress*, was Willet's response to Macartney's Stone Lecture at Princeton Seminary on that Christian classic; a companion window for the west reading room portrays Milton's *Paradise Lost.* (Among his many later commissions were windows

The Deal sisters had been parishioners of Dr. Clarence E. Macartney when he was pastor of the Arch Street Presbyterian Church in Philadelphia, and in gratitude for his ministry they provided funds for the library. He was the son of Professor John L. McCartney and grew up beside the Geneva campus. Later he was pastor of the First Presbyterian Church in Pittsburgh and Moderator of the General Assembly of the Presbyterian Church, USA, in 1924. It was Dr. Macartney's desire that the library be named for his family rather than for himself, hence the spelling of the name. The 1932 *Genevan.*

The library carillon has fourteen bells, ranging in size from 350 to 3,000 pounds, cast by the McShane foundry in Baltimore.

Left: The stained glass for the library was designed and crafted by Henry Lee Willet. This pane is a sample from the Willet window depicting *Pilgrim's Progress* and illustrates the opening words of Christian, "I dreamed a dream." The black and white outline unfortunately gives no suggestion of the vivid color in the windows.

at the National Cathedral in Washington and at the Chapel of the U. S. Military Academy at West Point.) The fourteen bells for the carillon were cast by the McShane bell foundry in Baltimore. The smallest bell is inscribed with the college motto, *Pro Christo et Patria.* Each of the others has two inscriptions, one from the Psalms and the other from "Ring Out, Wild Bells," a part of Tennyson's poem "In Memoriam." Again the college was indebted to Robert Clarke, both for his association with the donors and for the

taste he brought to the planning of the building. The library's move into its handsome new home was the occasion for the advent of the college's first professional librarian, Miriam Grosh. She used her professional skill well in enlarging the collection, cataloguing the books more effectively, and creating special collections, particularly the Covenanter Collection with its extensive holdings of Reformed Presbyterian research material.

The 1930s brought the end of the long Geneva tradition of the Adelphic and Aletheorian Societies, in some

regards the last ties with the Geneva that had relocated in Beaver Falls half a century earlier. When the society rooms in Old Main were remodeled to accommodate the Department of Business Administration, the change symbolized the growing importance of professional education in the college curriculum. The Department of Business Administration was begun in 1926 when the Chair of Commerce and Business was endowed in memory of William Myler, a prominent Beaver County businessman, by his widow. The new department joined the departments of Education and Engineering in providing training for specific vocations, and like those departments it grew rapidly. A new degree, the Bachelor of Science in Business Administration, was created for the new program and first granted in 1930 to twelve students. Still, despite the popularity of the new degrees in education and business administration, the bachelor of arts degree remained in the 1930s the most popular degree. Some students chose it because of the prestige of the liberal arts. But the B.A. curriculum served a vocational purpose, too, in preparing students to teach the "arts" courses such as English, history, and languages in secondary school.

Through all of this period the college was officially committed to the Christian faith, at a time when many denominational colleges were giving up compulsory chapel and Bible instruction. At Geneva the required daily chapel services continued. Bible courses—academically demanding and effectively taught—were required of all graduates. On Sabbath morning a devotional service led by a faculty member was held in the chapel before the worship services in the various churches. The

The library steps have been the setting for many photographs. This picture was taken from North Hall, a vantage point that no longer exists.

service was led by a faculty member and well-attended. One Sabbath evening a month the local Reformed Presbyterian congregations joined the college in a convocation service held in the chapel; Pearce's convocation sermons became a treasured part of student memories. Once a year, usually in the spring, Religious Emphasis Week brought a guest minister to chapel to present the gospel. The YMCA and the YWCA continued their activities, with more emphasis on the Christian faith than had been true two decades earlier. The two associations provided teachers and social events for a Sabbath school in the Eastvale community across the river from the college. The Christian Service

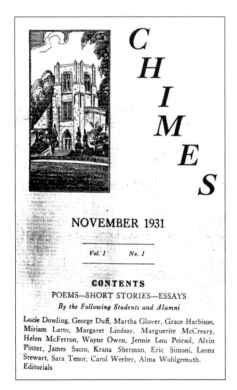

The college literary magazine, *The Chimes*, was founded in 1931. This is the cover of its first issue.

Until the construction of Memorial Hall, there was a park-like section of the campus behind Ferncliffe. Here students play badminton on what is now the lawn of Memorial Hall.

Union was organized for students interested in vocational service as pastors or missionaries.

But there were inconsistencies. Not all faculty members were sympathetic with the official religious stand of the college. Faculty members were required to be members of an "evangelical church," but often there was little inquiry beyond that formal requirement, and it was interpreted broadly. Nor did all students come because of the Christian commitment of the college; many came in spite of it, and were restive under what they considered its restrictions. The sociology of Beaver County was one of several factors that contributed to that tension. What was in those days often called simply The Valley had been dramatically changed a generation earlier by the arrival of Big Steel. Major plants were built along the Ohio River in towns created for them—Ambridge, Aliquippa,

A group of engineering students practice their surveying skills. Notice the appearance of the college corner before the building of Alexander Hall in 1971.

and Midland. As the demand for labor brought migration into the region, Beaver County became a kaleidoscope of nationalities and religious traditions. Geneva was the only college in the county, and for many families it provided the only access to higher education. Geneva thus played an important role in the community, and its student body reflected the diversity of nationalities and religions. Almost inevitably the tension between a commitment to the beliefs and standards of the Reformed Presbyterian Church and an increasingly diverse faculty and student body created significant problems both for the students and for the administration.

The Freshman Handbook was prepared for freshmen as a service of the YMCA and the YWCA. It included a brief history of Geneva and described many college traditions, including songs and cheers. It provided information on the calendar and sports schedules for the year and listed local churches.

Sara Smith was the Queen of the May in 1931.

This 1943 photograph shows a group of the college faculty and staff. Front row, left to right: Elizabeth D. Johnston, piano; Robert Clarke, assistant to the president; Gyla MacDowell, English; President Pearce; Charles M. Lee, Latin and Greek. Second row: Lulu McKinney, registrar; Edna George, physical education; J. C. Twinem, education; William Cleland, physics; Robert Park, history. Third row: Georgiana Wylie, psychology; Marguerite McCreary, book store; James S. Martin, executive secretary; Fritz Schaal, buildings and grounds. Back row, Dorothy Peters, position unknown; John Coleman, political science; E. May Girvan, treasurer; A. C. Edgecombe, engineering. A number of faculty members were absent.

SEVEN

WAR AND PEACE

1940 — 1948

*"Her children wide-scattered are everywhere loyal
To Geneva, our country, and the right.*"

The 1940s began in the shadow of the spreading war in Europe. "Defense" became the watchword; all sorts of plans appeared for the "contingency" that the United States might become involved. One such plan was the Selective Service Act, passed in the fall of 1940; Geneva had the unhappy distinction of being the first western Pennsylvania college to lose a faculty member to the draft, when Edwin Clarke (later the president of the college) was called to the Army. Enrollment began to drop as young men went to the service and as increasing industrial production provided well-paid jobs as an attractive alternative to college. With the growing demand for skilled labor, the college offered engineering courses under the U.S. Engineering Defense Training Program, meeting in the evening and taught by college faculty and by engineers from local industry. Five hundred men participated in these courses. Groups of pilots were trained, their ground instruction given at Geneva, and their flying done at the Butler County Airport.

Suddenly with the attack on Pearl Harbor, December 7, 1941, the contingent became the real. The campus became global, as students, faculty, and alumni were drafted or volunteered and were sent to training camps across the United States and to combat around the world. As Dean Lee had conferred with students over their college problems, he now began to keep a record of where they were stationed. His notebook survives, with the names and addresses of 835 Genevans. As he heard news from them, he noted their injuries, their decorations, and, all too often, their deaths. The *Geneva Alumnus* expanded to include news and letters from servicemen and women around the world. The college calendar and courses were revised to meet the emergency needs of students still on campus. Geneva's first winter commencement, in 1943, allowed twenty-one students to finish their work and receive their diplomas six months ahead of schedule, before they entered the service.

The college offered its services to the government as it had in World War I, and it was chosen by the Army Air Force for the training of cadets. The campus was "invaded" by three hundred servicemen. The first contingent arrived

An aerial view shows the campus and its surrounding community, probably about 1945.

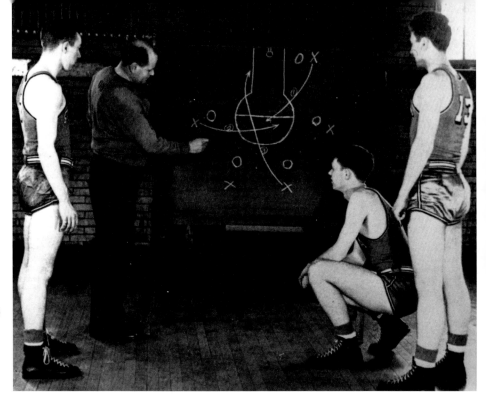

Basketball was the one intercollegiate sport played at Geneva during the Second World War. When Allured Ransom went to the service, Harold Bruce, professor of biology, became coach. He is here shown in a strategy session before a game. The 1944 *Genevan*.

You see boys in uniform on the campus. . . . By ones and twos and threes they come back—soldiers on furlough and sailors on leave—with various insignia on shoulders and collars and service stripes on their breasts that tell so little of what one would like to know. . . . When Dr. Pearce can get his hands on one of them, he coaxes him up to the rostrum at chapel time. The students sing a psalm and the President reads a chapter from the Bible. Then the man from a war-front is called upon for a speech. He looks down into faces that seem very young. The chapel hall is shrunken and strangely quiet. He tries to think of something to say, something interesting, pleasant, natural . . . and not heroic. War can be made interesting . . . at a distance. . . . It is very hard to know what to say. He stammers painfully, . . . and sits down, feeling damp and hot.

J. Vale Downie, the *Geneva Alumnus*, April, 1945.

ahead of schedule, early on the morning of February 27, 1943. Pearce described their arrival, "swinging up College Avenue from the railroad station singing their air corps song and letting the community know they were there." Relationships with the Air Force were happier than arrangements with the military in World War I; and for a year and a half, the presence of men in large numbers on the campus was welcomed. Income from that program allowed the college to restore the 15 percent by which salaries were cut during the Depression.

How was campus life affected by the war? Football, which had a winning 6-3 season under Coach Slim Ransom in 1942, was discontinued until 1946. Basketball continued through the war, with biology professor Harold Bruce as coach; he had winning seasons in his last two years. Other intercollegiate sports were cancelled. Students carried on the activities and traditions where they could: Homecoming, the all-school party, the Genevans (though with few tenors and basses), a swing band, *The Cabinet*, the *Genevan*, May Day in the

spring. But there were vivid reminders of the war. Mail was precious. Men and women on leave from the service brought the war onto the campus.

The first anniversary of Pearl Harbor was marked by an impressive service. Lt. Raymond Shotsinger, Class of 1937, had called on the Archbishop of Canterbury in London and asked him to inscribe a Bible for Geneva; it was formally presented to the college on December 7, 1942, with an address by Clarence Macartney. Tragically, Lt. Shotsinger was killed during the war.

The 1944 *Genevan* was dedicated to the Genevans in service:

Her children wide-scattered are everywhere loyal

To Geneva, our country, and the right.

These words taken from our Alma Mater are symbolic of the situation today. For "our children" are wide-scattered through all the sections of the globe . . . and they are fighting in the hope that we may all sing our Alma Mater together once again.

From February 1943 to June 1944, the facilities of the college were shared with cadets of the Army Air Force. They drilled on Reeves Field, lived in the dormitories, and took classes from Geneva faculty. The lounge in McKee Hall became an infirmary. The resident women on campus moved to houses on Park Place.

In the summer of 1945 came the hoped-for end of hostilities. Strangely, peace affected the college program more than war had. As men were discharged from the service they returned to college, aided financially by the G.I. Bill. The student body was soon twice as large as it had been before the war. Pearce commented to the board in his 1946 annual report:

We could hardly have foreseen the great inflow of students, the difficulties in securing teachers, the need for reconditioning our dormitories, the government's urgent call to crowd our classrooms, or the difficulty in securing materials for the addition [to the Science Hall] we planned. However, it is more desirable to be busy than to stand by and wait.

Half the students in college were veterans, many of them older than traditional college students and in a hurry to get through with their education and on with their lives. Pearce reported to the board in the spring of 1947:

You would be interested in my commenting on our experience with the veterans. . . . They are somewhat different from the usual college students and have both excellences and defects. One of the features which gave us immediate satisfaction with the veterans was the fact that they had gotten past the stage of foolishness which usually characterizes freshmen, and went about their

Fred Filippone, Geneva '41, wrote a song, "Moon on the Campus," which for a generation was a great campus favorite. The 1943 *Genevan*.

The Moon on the Campus

My heart lives again,
Tonight by Old Main,
'Neath the Moon on the campus ground;
Where once more I'll dream
Of a face in the beam,
Of the moon on the campus ground.
In years to be, I'll always see
One girl I'll love forever,
The girl with the "G",
Who waited for me
'Neath the moon on the Campus Ground

Words and music by Fred Filippone,
Class of '41

work seriously and generally with a definite purpose. They are as a group rather above the average as students. One adverse feature, however, which gradually came into view was the fact that they did not enter largely or freely into college activities outside the classroom. Many of them seem to come somewhat reluctantly to the required college work, and fail to show much of what we are accustomed to call "college spirit."

The veterans were older, many of them married and with families, working to supplement their benefits. Naturally the traditional college life was not for them.

But this was not the whole picture. To glance through the *Genevans* of those postwar years is to be reminded of how many returning students took up their activities and responsibilities where they had left off when they went to war. Veterans back in college were busy with journalism, music, drama, clubs, gospel teams. A number of the veterans returned to the campus with deepened spiritual lives, and their presence affected the tone of the campus. The full

Patterson Lodge, built at the foot of Park Place by President W. P. Johnston, was remodeled for a student residence just before World War II. Mrs. Ava Allen Wylie was its respected and beloved housemother for some time after the war. Here she serves breakfast in bed to Robert Neisslein, one of her "boys." The 1946 *Genevan.*

Below: The formal Big Sister-Little Sister dinner in the dining room of McKee Hall is presided over by Mrs. Irene Saxton, the housemother, whose graciousness helped shape the spirit of campus life. The 1946 *Genevan.*

President Pearce presides over the centennial luncheon. To his right, Governor and Mrs. Duff; to his left, Dr. Clarence Macartney and Lincoln B. Hale, the president of Evansville College, who was the luncheon speaker.

In 1948 Geneva celebrated its one-hundredth birthday. The speaker for the occasion was the Honorable James Duff, governor of Pennsylvania. Here Twila Black, the 1948 May Queen, pins a carnation on Governor Duff.

In this photograph, a men's intramural game is in progress in the old field house.

Women's intramural games were played in Johnston Gym.

The "old" field house was constructed out of war surplus material from World War II. It stood on the site of the present field house. For ten years this building served as the center for men's athletics. The 1951 *Genevan.*

array of intercollegiate sports began again. Larry Bruno returned to play football and to give Geneva its first national recognition since the days of Bo McMillin. Golf, tennis, cross-country, and track teams reorganized. By 1947, of the twelve students chosen to *Who's Who in American Colleges and Universities* for their contributions to college life, five were back on campus from war service.

As the student body grew beyond the five hundred students typical before the war, the college needed more room. The first building project, begun while it was still difficult to find materials, was the modest 1948 addition to the east side of the Science Hall. An unexpected windfall came to the college as the government dismantled its wartime facilities and offered them to colleges hard-pressed by the sudden rise in enrollment. From that war surplus Geneva erected two buildings, happily temporary, but in their time very useful: a gymnasium built on the site of the present Field House and the small white Brigadoon on the site of the present Student Center. The Brig provided for the first time a spot on campus where students could "hang out" for a Coke and a sandwich. It was a special boon for commuters.

During this exciting time, with the enrollment growing beyond the imagination of a previous generation, the college celebrated its centennial. The formal commemoration came on the one hundredth birthday of the college, April 20, 1948. In the morning assembly Dr.

Clarence Macartney reviewed the history of Geneva. Born in Northwood and growing up on the edge of the campus in Beaver Falls, he had known many of the people who had shaped Geneva's life. The president of Evansville College, Lincoln B. Hale, spoke at the centennial luncheon. The academic procession in the afternoon included representatives from Harvard, Yale, and Princeton, as well as from many colleges with special ties to Geneva, who came to offer their congratulations. The address on that notable occasion was given by Pennsylvania Governor James Duff, whose roots in Pittsburgh had given him personal connections with Reformed Presbyterians.

Later, during commencement week in May, the celebration was climaxed with an impressive pageant in Reeves Field reliving many incidents in the history of the college.

That fall of 1948, after the commemoration of the centennial, the campus was stunned by the sudden death of President Pearce on November 22. The thirteenth president, his administration had spanned a quarter of Geneva's century, through depression, war, and peace. Most of the college family had known no other president. God had graciously allowed him before his death both to celebrate Geneva's past and to see the bright prospects for its future.

Freshmen were welcomed into the Geneva student body through suffering a number of indignities. Dressing in some ridiculous and embarrassing way was usually part of the process. The 1936 *Genevan*.

One of the annual freshman chores was to clean the college sign with tooth-brushes. The 1946 *Genevan*.

EIGHT

PLANNING FOR THE FUTURE

1948 — 1960

♠

"   *Since [to glorify God] is the chief purpose of life,
it is also the chief purpose of education. . . .*   *"*

At its first meeting after Pearce's death, the Board of Trustees asked the dean of the college, Charles M. Lee, to serve as Acting President. As dean, Lee had been a central figure in the Pearce administration, and there was a smooth transition. After a successful year, the board elected him president, and his inauguration was held on Founders Day, April 20, 1950. His undergraduate training had been at The College of Wooster and Miami University in Ohio. He studied for a year in Rome, and received his Ph.D. in classics from the University of Pittsburgh. He joined the Geneva faculty in 1918 and had served as dean of the college since 1925.

One immediate decision confronting the new president was a replacement for the men's dormitory, North Hall. This 1888 building, located between Old Main and McCartney Library, had been the women's dormitory until McKee Hall was built. It was not in good repair; and in any case the college urgently needed a larger

building for the growing number of resident men. The obvious location for a new dormitory was the space north of Ferncliffe, overlooking the river. Arthur

The Brigadoon was built in 1950 and at once became a popular meeting spot for commuters and dorm students. It was named for the mythical village in the musical of the same name.

Left: President Charles Marston Lee Charles Marston Lee (1888–1982) served as president of Geneva from 1949 to 1956.

Martsolf was chosen as architect, and he presented an attractive plan to the trustees, designed to be a companion dormitory to McKee Hall. Before starting on the project the trustees had planned its financing, but the bids that came in shocked the board, $150,000 more than the $250,000 they thought it possible to raise.

The new dormitory was clearly a necessity, but it would be possible only with vigorous fundraising. Robert Clarke, who had dealt with such situations for forty years, was now in his eighties. Lee had indicated that with his academic responsibilities as president, he could not spend time fundraising. To find the necessary capital funds the board elected Edwin Clarke, head of the Economics Department, to succeed his father as fundraiser and gave him the title of vice president. With Clarke's confidence that the necessary $400,000 could be raised, the board gratefully approved the construction. The building was named

The Brig was a busy place. The 1958 *Genevan*.

Memorial Hall, primarily in honor of Geneva's men and women who served in World War II. Memorial rooms in the building also honored many other members of the Geneva family. The building was opened to students in the fall of 1952. (For $1,750 North Hall was razed, the spot graded and seeded, the place where once it stood barely remembered even by the old-timers! The north campus could at last take the form Robert Clarke had envisioned for it when McKee Hall was built thirty years before.)

Memorial Hall, a men's dormitory, was named to honor the Geneva men and women who served in the armed forces during World War II.

The middle 1950s marked the retirement or death of a group of faculty members who had shaped the life of the college for a quarter-century: J. Boyd Tweed in Bible, Georgiana Wylie in psychology, John Coleman in Bible and political science, Philip Coon in chemistry, J. C. Twinem in education, Robert Park in history, William Cleland in physics, President Lee in the classics. Somehow, in class and out of class, they were the college, making it what it was and influencing the lives of the students whom they taught. Inevitably some of the flavor of Geneva left with them. But as they left, other professors joined the faculty and stamped their mark on the college and its students: Johannes Vos in

Ground was broken for Memorial Hall April 3, 1951. On the platform were representatives of the services: William Dolan of the U.S. Army; Martin McCullough of the U.S. Navy; Robert Knight of the U.S. Marine Corps; and John Heller of the U.S. Air Corps. President Lee is presiding. To his right is Robert M. Young, president of the Board of Trustees, who delivered the address.

These pictures record the razing of North Hall in 1952. It was built as a women's dormitory in 1888. After the opening of McKee Hall for women, it became a men's dormitory and was renamed North Hall. Its disappearance opened up the north campus, creating a more appropriate setting for McCartney Library.

Johannes G. Vos served as chairman of the Bible Department from 1954 to 1974. His widely read writings in Reformed theology brought new visibility to Geneva.

Leotta Caldwell Hawthorne was an inspiration to education students; a garden at the entrance to McCartney Library is a memorial to her influence in their lives. The *Genevan.*

Janet Metheny Downie

Janet Metheny Downie edited the *Geneva Alumnus* from 1945 until 1958 and for the last ten of those years served also as director of public relations. Her husband, James Vale Downie, served as assistant editor for much of that time, contributing his witty essays, many of them on Geneva history. The Downies, of the Geneva Class of 1905, came from Geneva families, lived near the campus, and were deeply involved in the life of the college. Their friendship and the openness of their home enriched the memories of many Genevans. The 1955 *Genevan.*

One of Geneva's great teachers, John Coleman taught the required course in political science from 1921 to 1954. The course focused largely on American government, but always in the light of his concern that the government ought to be confessedly Christian. He was one of a number of senior faculty members who retired or died in the middle 1950s. The 1954 *Genevan.*

Bible, Roy Adams in chemistry, Theodore McMillion in biology, Elizabeth Douglas in art and humanities, Ann Paton and Norman Carson in English, Stewart Lee in economics, Leotta Hawthorne in education—a sampling of the influential teachers of the next generation.

The 1950s were glory days for basketball. Clifford Aultman, one of Geneva's outstanding athletes (as a student he won fifteen letters in four sports), returned to his Alma Mater to coach. For four consecutive years beginning in 1953 Geneva won the state National Association of Intercollegiate Athletics title; as much of the campus as could traveled to Kansas City to watch the team play in the national NAIA tournament. A mark of the respect in which Aultman was held beyond the campus came when the U.S. Department of State selected him to coach the Indonesian basketball team for the All-Asia Games in Tokyo. Football was revived after World War II. Under coaches Ransom, West, and Morgan, the team did well, with nine winning seasons during fourteen years. (It was also during this period that Geneva sustained its worst defeat, losing to West Virginia 89-0!) The cross-country team won district championships in 1954, 1955, and 1960, with Robert Park still serving as coach.

Above: Clifford Aultman was one of Geneva's greatest athletes in his student days in the 1930s. He returned to Geneva as athletic director and basketball coach. He led his team to four straight Pennsylvania NAIA championships from 1953 to 1957.

Left: Bill Blair's career scoring record of 2,052 points from 1953 to 1957 stood for twenty-two years. His season scoring record of 739 points in 1953–1954 stood for twenty-four years.

During the mid-fifties the Board of Trustees took two actions that were significant in the history of the college. In October 1956, the trustees received, discussed, and adopted the report of a board committee chaired by Remo Robb, Home Missions and Young Peoples' Secretary for the Reformed Presbyterian Synod. The committee had been appointed to review the objectives of the college and to assess how well those objectives were being met. The committee's report restated clearly the long-held position of the college: a commitment to be a Christian college, a commitment to a Reformed understanding of the Christian faith, and a commitment to the principles of the Reformed Presbyterian Church. But the report also recognized that "a generation has grown to college age with little awareness . . . of the vital place of Jesus Christ in their lives and life plans." How could the commitment of the college be made meaningful to a student body many of whom did not share that commitment? The committee made specific proposals regarding faculty selection and student recruitment, and it asked the administration to promote a more pervasive Christian atmosphere in the curriculum and on the campus. The report provided the context for a number of changes in the life of the college that came later.

A second important decision of the period was the commissioning of a

The Geneva steamroller rolled in the Homecoming Parade of 1954. (Unfortunately the hopes of the float-builders did not come true—Westminster defeated Geneva 8-0.)

master plan for the college from the firm of Michael Baker, Jr., Engineering, Inc. In its first report to the board in the spring of 1956, the Baker firm noted that 75 percent of the day school students came from within twenty-five miles of the college and 90 percent from Pennsylvania. Assuming the continued demand for a college education in American society and in the then-prosperous local area, the college could expect to grow. The first question was how large a college the board would like to see. Once that decision was made, it would be possible to plan for classrooms, dormitories, auxiliary buildings, and parking space; and to estimate costs and consider methods of financing. After

much discussion, the board agreed that it would plan for a college of one thousand full-time day school students in twelve years. This was about the size the college had been at the postwar peak, about 20 percent larger than it was as the report was being considered. At a later meeting, the Baker firm displayed a topographic model of proposed campus development for a thousand-member student body, with suggested buildings and floor plans. In the fall of 1956, the Baker plan was adopted by the Board of Trustees as a

Doris Nevin taught physical education at Geneva from 1948 to 1959. Though there were then no organized intercollegiate sports for women, she had an infectious enthusiasm that made on-campus sports important for Geneva women. The May Day programs she directed were highlights of the college year. The 1956 *Genevan* was dedicated to her, noting especially her "wonderful Christian attitude." The 1956 *Genevan*.

Below: Albert Miller, Geneva drum major, was named national champion in 1950 in a contest at the University of Michigan. The 1951 *Genevan*.

Bonnie Heather of Geneva, a Scotch terrier, first appeared as the Geneva mascot in the Homecoming Parade of 1951.

The members of the Buildings and Grounds staff posed for a picture for the 1954 *Genevan*. One especially well-remembered figure is Sam Edgar, who for years was the custodian of the library and distributor of "Sam's Sweepings," an occasional collection of wise and witty sayings.

general guide for campus expansion. Its adoption set the board on a "growth mode" for both enrollment and facilities.

Things happening outside the campus later modified those plans. One tiny item appeared in the minutes of the Board of Trustees: there was word early in 1956 that Penn State University was considering a plan to establish a technical institute in the area. That proposal did not materialize, but it foreshadowed the time when there would be in the community a number of alternate sources for a college education. When that occurred a decade later in the 1960s, the new environment had a significant effect, both frightening and freeing, for Geneva.

Geneva had been accredited in 1922 by the Middle States Association. The Association had apparently not reviewed that accreditation for more than thirty years, the decades of the depression, World War II, and the enormous growth of college enrollment after the war. Obviously, a review was appropriate. The association scheduled a visit to Geneva and asked the college to prepare for that visit by doing a self-evaluation. In February 1956, a team visited the

In 1953 Frances Gilchrist (McCracken) was crowned Queen of the May. Here Queen Frances stands between her attendants, Pat Farls (Baumann) and Wilma Kohne (Murphy). The last Geneva May Queen was crowned in 1971. The next year, with a new calendar, commencement came early in May and the tradition was discontinued. The 1953 *Genevan*.

Students gathered daily for worship in the chapel, which would then still accommodate the whole student body. Here J. Boyd Tweed, professor of Bible, is speaking. President Lee is presiding. Seated beyond Professor Tweed is Philip Coon, professor of chemistry, who led in the singing of the Psalms.

After chapel, which was then held in mid-morning, the Old Main stairs were jammed on the way down to the lobby. Everyone congregated there, socialized there, and there the morning mail was distributed. The 1937 *Genevan*. The 1946 *Genevan*.

college, examined it in the light of the self-study, and made its report. The association expressed concerns about the academic qualifications, salaries, and teaching loads of the faculty; the selection process for students; and the administrative structure of the college. It asked Geneva to do a new self-study in preparation for a follow-up visit in two years.

During this period of substantial change at Geneva, President Lee submitted his resignation to the Board of Trustees at its meeting in October 1956. He had served the college for thirty-eight years: he taught classical languages (and on occasion other subjects—his learning was broad); he was chosen secretary of

Accreditation

In the system of American higher education, colleges are autonomous agencies. The accreditation process presents some challenge to that autonomy. At the same time it forces a college to examine itself, to some extent against outside measures. Shortcomings that tradition or complacency have made familiar or that lack of resources seem to make necessary have to be laid out for review. The accrediting agency has no direct control over the college; but loss of accreditation is a serious challenge to the college's ability to survive.

the faculty; as dean he had counseled hundreds of students and parents. For seven years he was president. The Board of Trustees accepted his resignation, expressing its appreciation for his long and faithful service to Geneva.

Vice president Edwin C. Clarke was chosen to succeed Lee as president. His

President Lee is pictured here with J. Merrill Robb, who was president of the Board of Trustees for twenty-eight years from 1953 to 1981.

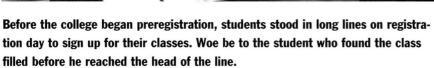

Before the college began preregistration, students stood in long lines on registration day to sign up for their classes. Woe be to the student who found the class filled before he reached the head of the line.

Two of the major buildings on the campus were under construction at the same time. The Student Center was replacing the small frame Brigadoon, and the Science Hall was being expanded to become the Science and Engineering Building.

formal inauguration came October 12, 1957, with the inaugural address by John Dale Russell of the University of Chicago, a specialist in the field of college administration and long a friend of Geneva.

During the opening years of his presidency, Clarke gave special attention to three areas. An immediate concern was to respond to the report of the Middle States Association. He worked to reduce faculty teaching loads. He initiated a sabbatical program that encouraged faculty members to finish requirements for their doctorates. He included in the college budget stipends for study during the summer and financial help in the research necessary for Ph.D. dissertations. Under Clarke, the college received a $155,000 grant from the Ford Foundation to raise faculty salaries. To reinforce its position as a liberal arts college, Geneva added a requirement in the humanities for graduation. It began to require applicants to submit their Scholastic Aptitude Test scores for admission. Clarke reorganized the administrative structure of the college, creating the President's

Cabinet. Five administrative officials—the academic dean, the business manager, the director of public relations and development, the director of student affairs, and the director of spiritual activities—were named to it, and he invited the faculty to elect two of its members to serve on it.

The team from the Middle States Association that made an interim visit in 1958 was encouraging in its assessment. In connection with that visit, representatives of the American Chemical Society reviewed Geneva's program in chemistry and granted that program a coveted Accreditation in Professional Training. In 1960, the accreditation of the college was reaffirmed by the Middle States Association.

A second major concern of Clarke's beginning years was the continued physical expansion of the campus. It was the need for such expansion that occasioned his election as vice president in 1950 and the erection of Memorial Hall. The Baker Master Plan of 1956 had indicated the need for a number of new buildings. After discussing priorities, the board selected two projects. One project

was an addition to the south side of the Science Hall, much needed as the science and engineering program had outgrown both the original building and the small eastward extension of 1948. The other was the construction of a new field house to replace the decaying war-surplus building that was making do as a center of men's athletics. Joseph Bontempo was selected as the architect for the field house, the first of several buildings that he would design for the campus. It was completed in the spring of 1961 and named the Metheny Field House in memory of C. Brainerd Metheny, Class of 1911, athletic director and coach before World War I, and for many years a member of the Board of Trustees.

Concurrently the federal government began to recognize that colleges needed capital to expand their physical plants as their enrollments grew. Geneva was able to secure loans to build two dormitories, named in memory of two beloved Geneva administrators, M. M. Pearce and Robert Clarke. Pearce Hall and Clarke Hall were dedicated in 1961. At the same time, the dining room and

Two new dormitories were constructed in 1961 to house the increasing resident population. A third floor was added to each in 1964. They were named for President M. M. Pearce and for Robert Clarke, whose title was Assistant to the President.

kitchen on the ground floor of McKee Hall were enlarged to accommodate the growing resident population.

In addition to rising academic standards and a growing physical plant, there was a third area of change at Geneva in late 1950s to which Clarke gave his steady support. This was an intensified effort by Geneva to be what John Black Johnston in 1848 had established it to be: a Christian college. In his inaugural address, Clarke described his ideal for the educational program at Geneva, "basically and essentially Christian in character, primarily liberal arts in nature, and excellent in quality." In discussing the first of those essentials, he said:

Since [to glorify God] is the chief purpose of life, it is also the chief purpose of education. . . . By Christian education we do not mean secular education with Christian features added externally; Christian education means education that is Christian in its essence. . . . The Bible, as the revelation of the mind and will of God, is the true standard of education and therefore the relevant principles of the Bible are the standard for every field of

study. It is not by accident that the open Bible has been placed in the center of the Geneva College seal. Since we recognize this unifying principle to true education, no part of knowledge will be properly taught unless this relationship is assumed, and so far as is appropriate, pointed out.

The Robb report adopted by the trustees in 1956 provided both support and direction for the principles Clarke here expressed.

The most immediate and tangible changes came in those areas that Clarke had called "external," but externals that were essential to the spirit of the college, such matters as daily chapel and Spiritual Emphasis Week. He created the position of Director of Spiritual Activities and included the director in his cabinet. Clarke appointed Willard McMillan of the Bible department to be the first director. McMillan brought both skill and commitment to the position. Under his leadership chapel programs changed. For many years, chapel had begun with an often perfunctory time of singing, scripture reading, a short devotional message, and prayer, but it served chiefly for announcements, pep rallies,

and skits advertising various campus activities. McMillan brought to chapel services a new spirit of worship.

Spiritual Emphasis Week, when a visiting minister came to speak in chapel, was taken more seriously, with the campus community meeting for prayer in preparation for the services. In 1962, Calvin Malefyt, pastor of the University Reformed Church of Ann Arbor, Michigan, was the week's speaker. He not only spoke in chapel, but also made himself available for speaking in dorms, counseling, meeting with small groups late into the night. His visit made a dramatic impact on the campus, and Spiritual Emphasis Week gained a new format. McMillan and the chairman of the Spiritual Resources Committee of the Board of Trustees, J. Paul McCracken, met with small groups on the campus for prayer and Bible study. Professor Charles McBurney organized the Christian Student Fellowship choir to present John and Mary Coleman's *Christ in the Psalms*, which combined selections from the gospels with the singing of the Messianic prophecies from the Psalms. Later, the same choir presented

The Christian Student Fellowship Choir poses for a yearbook photo. The 1966 *Genevan*.

Out of Egypt and *Witnesses Unto Me*, arranged by McBurney. These were all hopeful signs of spiritual renewal.

Charles McBurney came to Geneva to teach political science; later he was appointed director of admissions, where he changed the recruitment focus of Geneva. One of his unofficial contributions was to organize the Christian Student Fellowship Choir, which presented programs telling the story of the Bible through the Psalms. The 1963 *Genevan*.

NINE

A SENSE OF IDENTITY

1960 — 1970

The physical expansion of the campus in the 1960s was occurring at a time when all colleges were moving into an uncertain terrain. . . .

During the 1960s the expansion of the campus facilities continued. There was a carefully planned expansion to McCartney Library, adding stack space to house its growing collection and additional office space for the staff, but keeping the high-ceilinged Gothic reading rooms intact. On Geneva's 118th birthday, April 20, 1966, the new facilities were dedicated. Sadly, Eleanor Leighty, long the librarian, died just as the library began to use the new facilities she had helped design.

The Science Hall became the Science and Engineering Building. The old 1897/1913 building was hardly recognizable after it was renovated and surrounded by a new structure that quadrupled its original size. There were now laboratories for the complex experiments of a more sophisticated curriculum, space for the computers that were appearing, and classrooms into which non-science classes overflowed as the curriculum and the student population outgrew Old Main. The changes in and additions to the building were made in three stages.

This is an unusual view of the Student Center. The windows on its upper stories provide especially vivid views on October days.

President Edwin Cameron Clarke Edwin Cameron Clarke (1913–1987) was president from 1956 to 1980. He returned as acting president in 1983–84. The 1965 *Genevan*.

The first section was dedicated in 1965 and sections two and three in 1969.

To accommodate the increasing resident population of the college, a new floor was added to each of the new residence halls, Pearce and Clarke, for the opening of school in 1964. There was serious planning for another major residence building, with several possibilities of design and location considered. One proposal was a twelve-story circular tower, to be located north of Clarke Hall, an option considered and rejected. In the midst of that planning, the college was able instead to acquire Geneva Arms, a nearby apartment complex built in 1966 on the site of the old College Hill reservoir. It was purchased in 1968. Part of the building was renamed Young Hall, in memory of Robert M. Young, a trustee from 1918 to 1969 and president of the board for thirty-two of those years. For the first year, one hundred students were housed in Young Hall; the rest of the buildings continued to provide convenient apartments for local residents. Gradually

The new Student Center was dedicated in October 1966. The 1966 *Genevan*.

Richardson House is the official residence for the college president.

The "new" Brig in the Student Center at once became a major gathering place for commuters, dorm students, and faculty.

more of the complex was used by the college until in 1996 all the apartments were occupied by students.

As other property near the campus became available, the college acquired it. Several of the private dwellings were used as student residences. What these houses lacked in facilities, they provided in fellowship. With the costs of upkeep, utilities, and supervision, they were not economical, and by the 1990s most of the buildings had been razed; but many Genevans look back with pleasure on the close friendships formed in that environment.

As the campus expanded, it surrounded Ferncliffe, where President and Mrs. Pearce lived during his presidency. By 1961, there were dormitories around it, and it had lost the privacy the Pearces had enjoyed. So to provide a residence for the president, the college acquired and remodeled Richardson House in 1964. The Clarkes and their successors have used it graciously as a setting for many college events.

This was also the period of the Old Main stairwells! The country had been sensitized to safety by a disastrous school fire in Chicago, and public buildings were widely scrutinized for unsafe conditions. In Old Main the long wooden staircases with their tempting bannisters were part of Geneva tradition, but they were indeed a fire hazard as the exit from the chapel and classrooms on the upper floors. The authorities, following the rule to the letter, required that fireproof stairwells be constructed at the longest dimensions of the building. This meant that there must be a stairwell behind the chapel stage, though this was obviously not a traffic area. But regulations were regulations! So a new stairwell was erected behind the chapel, and a wide corridor was cut through the stage for access to it. For a quarter of a century, until the remodeling of the chapel in the 1980s, Geneva could make a unique, if unhappy, claim to having the only known stage divided by a six-foot gap.

A new center for student activity, to replace the small Brigadoon, had long been the dream of Dean of Students Harold Bruce. In planning for the building, he visited student centers at other colleges to study the design and function which would best suit Geneva's

Professor Ann Paton. The 1971 *Genevan.*

Professor Howard Mattsson-Bozé. The 1970 *Genevan.*

Professor Elizabeth Douglas.

In 1969 Geneva introduced the humanities sequence as part of its core requirement. The four-course unit was designed to expose the students to the arts and to relate the arts to the world and life view that they presented. These are three members of the team that developed the course and taught it.

campus and students. It was he who insisted on the site overlooking the Beaver River, recognizing that the view from its balconies would be dramatic, especially during a Pennsylvania fall. It was therefore appropriate that the building had an autumn dedication in October 1965. The building housed an enlarged Brigadoon for meals and snacks, rooms for leisure activities, the campus store, bowling lanes, and the most popular spot on campus (at least for resident students): the mailboxes. The area between Old Main and the Student Center was landscaped to provide a plaza that became the cross-roads of the campus.

During the 1960s, Clarke appointed two officers who were central in his administration. Since 1961, Charles O'Data has been one of the significant figures in the life of the college. After serving in public relations and as alumni secretary, O'Data was named in 1967 as Director of Development (later Vice President for Development). During his tenure in that office, he has had a variety of responsibilities, including the athletic program and student recruit-

ment. But of course central to his position was the responsibility to provide the financial resources necessary for the college: unrestricted giving to keep the operating budget in balance; and capital funds to maintain and expand the academic programs and physical facilities of the college.

In 1963, William Russell, professor of history, was named academic dean. He served in that office until 1985, during a period when academic standards of the faculty were being raised. With his encouragement and assistance, many faculty members were able to complete the requirements for the Ph.D. degree, and the percentage of Geneva faculty with that degree rose steadily. With the adoption of the *Foundational Concepts of Christian Education*, Russell became responsible for implementing its academic implications: to attract faculty who shared the commitment expressed in that document; and to encourage changes in the curriculum and teaching that would reflect its principles more effectively.

On campus, the 1950s and 1960s were the golden age for clubs. There were clubs related to the curriculum, where students could expand their experience outside the classroom, performing plays in French, tasting Spanish cuisine, hearing speakers on economics. There were pre-professional clubs, where students could meet people in the profession, take field trips, and get a taste of what the profession would be like. There were activity clubs for acting, debating, making music. There were clubs for hobbies, like chess. There were organizations for student publications. There were clubs honoring students who had earned letters in athletics. There were all-campus groups responsible for student government and activities. These clubs also served many functions beyond their stated purposes: from their club experiences students learned how to work together, often under pressure; they developed management skills; they made close friends; and they escaped from the routine of classes.

In 1968, the college acquired an apartment complex near the campus, named Geneva Arms, for student housing. For some time tenants from the community continued to have apartments there, including Geneva alumni and friends who enjoyed being close to campus activities. In 1996 the last of the building was taken over for students.

The physical expansion of the campus in the 1960s was occurring at a time when all colleges were moving into an uncertain terrain: Would the demand for college education continue to grow? What sorts of colleges would supply the demand? What was the outlook for private colleges? How could rising capital costs and operating expenses be provided? The Baker Master Plan of 1956 and the college planning associated with it had projected the possibility of modest growth as a framework for Geneva's decision-making. But the outlook for private colleges kept changing. In the early 1960s a new Long Range Planning Committee described the pressure on Geneva to grow more

On April Fool's Day, 1971, the students demonstrated their "widened outlook" in the humanities classroom. The 1971 *Genevan*.

rapidly. The number of students graduating from Beaver County high schools would be up by 37 percent in two years. The college could increase enrollment sharply if it chose, and other institutions would respond to the opportunity if Geneva did not. The report stated that with its existing staff and facilities the college could accommodate two hundred students more than its existing enrollment of one thousand. However, that figure could not meet the predicted demand for college admission from the immediate area. On the basis of the committee's report, Clarke recommended planning toward a student body of fifteen hundred, of whom 57 percent would be commuters. At that level prospective applicants from Beaver County could be accommodated, if not in day school at least in evening school.

Just as these statistics were being pondered, the terrain began to shift again. The demand for college education was putting pressure on government agencies to provide publicly funded facilities. By 1967, the county had two junior colleges, the Beaver campus of Pennsylvania State University and the Community College of Beaver County; and the once-private University of Pittsburgh had become semi-public, subsidized by the state so that it could substantially lower its tuition. Geneva developed good relationships with its two new neighbors in the county. For some years the faculties of the three colleges met annually to get acquainted, attend seminars, and hear well-known speakers. Geneva worked hard to attract students who had completed their associate degrees at Penn State Beaver or at CCBC.

But clearly this development changed the planning terrain for Geneva. By the end of the decade Geneva's enrollment was slowly declining rather than rising. Even a slow decline was financially significant because the fixed costs of the college were high. Early in 1968, Clarke described the financial situation of the college to the trustees in unusual detail and called the short-run financial situation "alarming."

Meanwhile other changes were taking place that dramatically affected the future. One change was the decision to pursue the work of the Robb committee from the 1950s on the aims and purposes of Geneva. The Board of Trustees, as part of a new financial campaign in the early 1960s, asked the Board of Corporators to approve the request for a major contribution from the denomination. In granting that request, the Corporators asked the 1964 Synod to direct the two boards, Corporators and Trustees, to appoint a joint committee to:

Study in depth the problems of implementing the distinctively Christian witness and character of Geneva College and to make recommendations to both boards and to Synod for developing this witness and character to its fullest degree.

James D. Carson, president of the Board of Corporators, was named chairman, and each board appointed three members. The corporators chosen to serve were Kenneth G. Smith, John H. White, and Paul D. McCracken. (McCracken soon moved to California and John O. Edgar replaced him.) The trustees on the committee were J. Merrill Robb, Jean L. Hemphill, and J. Renwick Patterson. The committee set out to

Three Geneva physicists: John Pinkerton, John Schaefer, and Charles Fuget.

Below: Paul Arnold taught the first computer class offered at Geneva. He is here shown with students looking at Geneva's first computer, an IBM 1130. The *Genevan*.

define a philosophy of Christian higher education that would express the "idea" of Geneva. As that statement took shape, the committee then considered how such a philosophy might be implemented in the choice of college personnel and the admission of students. The committee worked with the administration and the faculty both in defining the philosophy and in proposing methods of implementation. Drafts were circulated and discussed by both boards and by the college faculty and administration. The document that emerged, *Foundational Concepts of Christian Education*, described what Geneva was, and what it hoped to become. It was adopted by Synod and by the Board of Trustees in 1967.

Starting with the belief that God is the source of all truth, education becomes the exciting adventure of seeking to appropriate knowledge in all its various facets under the guidance of the Holy Spirit. . . . While education in a Christian context does not guarantee truth, it does seek to establish the starting point apart from which ultimate truth can never be learned.

from the preface to *Foundational Concepts of Christian Education*.

The document described the foundation of a Geneva education in Reformed theology, as summarized in the *Westminster Confession of Faith*. Given that view of God and of the world, the document stated the purpose of higher education and the implications of such an education for the institution, for the student, for the curriculum, and for the exercise of discipline. Finally, in separate sections, the document made recommendations for implementation in the two specific areas of personnel and admissions. Implementing the *Foundational Concepts* was not easy for the college, as it drew lines in theology and in Christian commitment that were not new but had not previously been clearly articulated. As the committee remarked in its first report, "To say that Geneva

Roy Adams joined the Geneva faculty in 1946. He served as chairman of the Chemistry Department from 1954 to 1985 and continues to teach in the chemical engineering program. He is a recognized authority on boron chemistry, and from 1965 to 1975 he served as the U.S. representative on the Nomenclature Commission of the International Union of Pure and Applied Chemistry. He is joined here by his Geneva colleagues, Martin Price, Kenneth Hartman, and David Badger.

From its beginning in an attic along Park Place, WGEV provided hands-on experience in the many phases of operating a radio station. About 1970 it got its own building. One of its faculty directors, Mike Emrick, later became the Voice of the Philadelphia Flyers and official sportscaster for Olympic hockey games in 1992 and 1996.

The Bagpiper Theater began life as an Isaly's store, part of the once well-known ice-cream chain, and served as an informal social center on the edge of the campus. In 1966 it was remodeled to serve as a temporary theater. Despite its limited facilities and intimate space, it has been the home of many exciting productions.

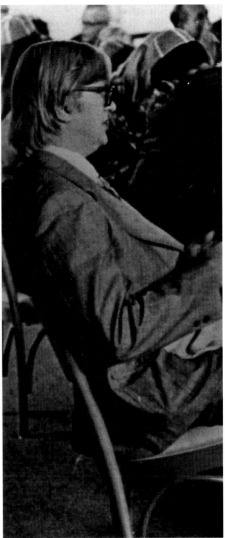

has had no philosophy would indeed be inaccurate, but nonetheless it remains that no formalized statement appears in her official documents to articulate her philosophy of Christian education." However, as the college worked through the process, it developed a sense of identity it had not possessed before.

The *Foundational Concepts*, printed in each college catalogue and widely circulated, attracted faculty members and students who wanted to teach and learn in such an environment. Faculty members, stimulated by that renewed focus, set about understanding more fully how their Christian faith affected their subject matter and their teaching. In 1966, President Clarke appointed Theodore McMillion, Ann Paton, and Arthur Fleser as a faculty committee to consider the implications of the *Foundational Concepts* for the curriculum. One concept that emerged from their discussions was that the arts of an era will express its view of God, man, and the universe. From this concept grew a pioneering venture, unique to Geneva. Faculty members from history, literature, the visual arts, and music worked

together to create and teach courses covering four semesters, in which students examined the arts in historical setting and pondered how those arts reflected the dominant world and life view. This "Humanities" sequence was introduced in 1969 and continues as a part of the required core. Another innovation was an annual lectureship on "The Christian Faith and the Arts," which for some years brought distinguished Christian artists to perform, read, exhibit; and in addition to speak about how their art reflected their faith in Jesus Christ.

Attempting to understand and to teach in the framework of a Christian world view was (and is) a complex and difficult task, and not without its tensions. In 1969, Peter Steen joined the faculty to teach philosophy. He was an outspoken teacher and faculty member, and he took every occasion to insist, not that the Christian faith and academic disciplines should interact with each other, but rather that all true learning must be dominated by Christian truth. An uninhibited scholar and intensely committed to a particular school of philosophy, he

Above: At least since 1969, African-Americans have had an organization at Geneva. They have broadened Geneva's cultural awareness, not least in the area of music. Here a black choir is rehearsing.

Right: The Gothic reading rooms in McCartney Library create an atmosphere conducive to study.

In 1948 the bell from the old college building in Northwood was brought from Ohio to Beaver Falls. After the Student Center was built it found a new home there. Here Virginia Montini (Humes), Carol McBurney (Lowe), Elizabeth Hutcheson, and Ed Miller are standing around the old bell. This is one of the few physical objects that connects the present with the earliest history of the college.

The Genevans were organized in 1938, combining the men's and women's glee clubs, which themselves had a long history. Here the Genevans and their director, Harold Greig, are pictured with Billy Graham in 1961 after they had sung for him on one of their spring tours to Florida.

found institutions confining, and predictably, for reasons doctrinal and personal, his contract was not renewed after his fourth year. But his years at Geneva left their mark on the institution: he had pushed both faculty and students to consider how to make all academic activity subject to a personal commitment to Jesus Christ as Savior and Lord and to the Biblical view of life.

While the college was defining its own character more clearly, God in His providence was providing a changing constituency for the college. A growing number of young people wanted a serious academic education that was not divorced from the historic Christian faith. Christian groups dealing with teenagers,

like Youth for Christ and Young Life, began searching for colleges they could recommend to their members. Christian higher education began to develop a sense of identity, symbolized by the creation of the Coalition of Christian Colleges, based in Washington D.C. As Geneva defined its own character more clearly, it became part of that identity, developing ties with theologically conservative Christians, those from Presbyterian and Reformed backgrounds and those from the broader evangelical world. Lee Troup, in his capacity as Geneva's Director of Public Relations, helped the college reach out to this new constituency, which began to discover Geneva and to appreciate the anchor for

Jesse Owens talks with President Clarke and Vice President for Development Charles O'Data, during Owens's visit to Geneva. Owens won four gold medals at the 1936 Olympics in Berlin, greatly angering Hitler.

faith and for Christian commitment that the *Foundational Concepts* provided. The hard work of Charles McBurney and Karl Cunningham as Directors of Admissions in changing the recruitment focus of the school provided more and more students who wanted the sort of Christian education Geneva set out to provide. The Christian faith became less a reason for apology and more a cause for gratitude and excitement.

As Geneva enrolled more students from this new constituency, its geographical range broadened. For many years, about two-thirds of Geneva students had commuted from their homes to the college; but by the late 1960s, 50 percent of the students lived on campus and by 1976 nearly 75 percent were resident students. This change in the campus population made a new dining hall necessary. It was completed for use in the fall of 1971 and was named for Ralph Alexander, Class of 1922, whose generosity helped make its construction possible. The dining hall was the last of the buildings erected in the major campus expansion of Clarke's administration. With its view from the dining room into trees of the campus, one trustee remarked at its opening, "It is a gracious place in which to be and to dine."

Paul Pupi was an outstanding scholar and athlete. He was three times named to the Little All-American Team. During his senior year in 1962, he was elected president of the Student Senate. Photograph courtesy of Dr. and Mrs. Paul Pupi.

The climax of the women's intramural basketball season was the selection of two teams, "Yale" and "Princeton," to play for the championship. The excitement of the occasion was increased by the faculty cheerleaders. The 1970 *Genevan*.

One of the winter social events was the crowning of the Basketball Queen. In 1966 Marjorie Dolanch was queen, with Beth Cross and Karen McKinney as her attendants.

Alexander Hall was completed in 1971 to serve as a dining hall for the increasing number of resident students. It was named for Ralph Alexander, of the Class of 1922. It also has provided office space for the departments of development and admissions.

Below: The cake is cut at the dedication of Alexander Hall. From left to right: Carl G. Baker, the architect; Carl Henning, president of the Student Senate; Willard McMillan, dean of students; Paul Cross of the Board of Trustees, who gave the dedicatory address; President Clarke; J. Merrill Robb, president of the Board of Trustees; John H. White, director of Spiritual Activities; Charles N. O'Data, vice president for development.

The plant of the Armstrong Cork Company adjoining the campus was established in 1903.

TEN

THE ENVIRONMENT CHANGES

1970 — 1980

❧

"❧*od and our fellow man and ourselves—these are the three dimensions of our*
    lives, and it is in relation to these that we develop our individuality. *"*

The late 1960s and the early 1970s were a "time of troubles" for American colleges. Agitation over the government's policy in Vietnam—and the "establishment" in general—became a challenge to authority on campuses across the country. Colleges, private or public, were not by nature democratic institutions; they were run by boards of trustees and administrators, typically with little official input from students. In a society that saw "democracy" as a good thing, the demand for "student power" over the circumstances of their education was not surprising.

Geneva did not experience the violent confrontations that many other campuses faced. Yet there were at Geneva those who questioned the status quo. Students asked for participation in, or at least communication about, college governance. The Student Senate, whose responsibilities had been largely social, now sought a voice in college policy. Some of the proposals it made did not

concern controversial issues—a new calendar, more available medical care and counseling, an evaluation of the core

When its plant beside the campus stopped operations, Armstrong World Industries presented the property to the college in two parts, in 1969 and 1974. Standing behind President Clarke are Lumley Wilson, representing the company; J. Merrill Robb, president of the Geneva Board of Trustees; Jon Trion from Armstrong; and Ralph Smith, the college attorney.

curriculum. And in fact the decade brought significant changes in these areas. But the Senate also raised more sensitive issues, which had been considered immune to change; for example, it questioned rules about behavior on campus, such as card-playing, smoking, and dancing. Most provocatively, the Student Senate presented to the administration for consideration by the trustees a "Student Bill of Rights," both its title and its tone a challenge to the traditional governance of the institution.

This was a new experience for both students and administrators. The methods of the students were at times confrontational, though never violent. Divergent points of view were vigorously aired in chapel and in *The Cabinet*. President Clarke noted to the trustees that some statements made in the minutes of the Student Senate and in *The Cabinet* were "disrespectful, some misleading, and some patently false." But he added:

Cork work smoke made Reeves Field look dark and gloomy on a winter day.

Reaction against the abusive statements made by a few students should not becloud the issues, and various requests which have been made deserve careful attention. . . . The Administration has no intention of abdicating its responsibility by yielding unwisely to student pressure. On the other hand we wish to remain sensitive to deserved criticism and constructive suggestions.

The administration responded cautiously in terms of power, as Clarke's statement suggested. But there were attempts at more open communication. The Student Senate was invited to lunch with the Board of Trustees. A proposal that two Senate representatives should attend board meetings was approved,

though never implemented. The Senate was asked to appoint student members to faculty committees and did so. Still, some students and faculty members were frustrated by the slowness of decision-making, by the difficulty of direct communication with the Board of Trustees, and by actions that seemed more symbolic than real. For example, the proposed "Student Bill of Rights," after several drafts and much discussion, seems to have died in a committee of the Board of Trustees.

At Geneva, because of its Christian commitment, there was an added component of the student mood, a desire to escape the conventions and proprieties that had rendered much American

Christianity bland and innocuous. There was a desire for a faith in Jesus Christ more clearly shown in love and concern, for more freedom and openness in living out that faith, and for more consistency between belief and behavior.

The most vivid expression of both aspects of the campus mood came in the *Genevan* revolution. Yearbooks had for years described themselves as chronicles of memories, and they had been. But the clear purpose of the 1971 *Genevan* was not to chronicle but to react, not to record events but to express feelings. Its title was chosen from C. S. Lewis's novel, *Till We Have Faces*, with the subtitle, *The Quest for Self-Identity*. There were many pictures of faces, no

After the college was given the Armstrong property, the extensive factory buildings were gradually demolished.

The Merriman Athletic Complex replaced the buildings of the "cork works."

Marshall Prentice, Rick Upton, and Steve Huggins of Geneva are competing against a runner from a visiting team in a cross-country race. Steve returned to the Geneva staff in 1976 and has served since as Director of Food Service. He has also coached winning cross-country teams for Geneva.

identifying captions, no narrative text, but brief quotations from varied sources. There were occasional musings:

Only to the degree to which we accept ourselves can we love other people. But, and it seems almost paradoxical, it is through our dealings with others and with God that we become aware of ourselves and are able to enjoy living with ourselves. God and our fellow man and ourselves—these are the three dimensions of our lives, and it is in relation to these that we develop our individuality.

The most dramatic yearbook of the period was the 1976 *Genevan*, a paperbound annual entitled "Distortion—76." This annual had a *great deal* of text along with its pictures, commenting at times straightforwardly, at times ironically, at times angrily on the year.

Student publications reflected at least some aspects of the tone on the campus. The first public expression at Geneva of reaction to the Vietnam War came on October 15, 1969. It began as a student proposal to wear blue arm bands to express general opposition to President Nixon's Vietnam policy, but

ended in some confusion: four different colors of arm bands appeared, and within those four groups there were varieties of opinion. Blue arm bands communicated varying degrees of opposition to government policy. Red-white-and-blue arm bands with a picture of a Vietnamese peasant represented support for the government, particularly to free the Vietnamese people from communism. White arm bands with red crosses said "Christ is the answer," though with different suggestions for implementing that slogan. The Black Union of Students wore black arm bands, protesting the disproportionate number of Blacks in the front lines in Vietnam. More than half of the students wore one of the four arm bands. The ensuing discussion was the most vigorous political expression heard up to that time on the Geneva campus.

The next spring, classes were cancelled on May 11 at the request of the Student Senate in memory of the four students killed at Kent State University the week before. Clarke reported to the trustees that about two hundred students had participated in the discussion groups

organized for the occasion. Faculty and others participated in a student-led candlelight vigil.

It is hard to know how widely the mood of challenge was shared on the campus. The caption for the picture of the Student Senate members in the 1974 *Genevan* stated sadly:

Not enough students appreciate how long and hard Senate works, but what's worse is that few care. No one need fear an outbreak of student activism at Geneva; what little interest that may be left can't survive much longer in the midst of such overwhelming apathy.

At the end of the 1970s, student leaders at Geneva were still expressing a persistent sense that they were unduly excluded from the communication process. But as elsewhere on college campuses, the Geneva mood was becoming more passive, forsaking the concern for public issues that had marked student life a decade before.

The glare of publicity in which American colleges lived during the 1970s, combined with the increasing sensitivity to bias in American society, led government agencies to concern

Above: Bill (Boomer) Aultman stands with his father, Cliff Aultman, and President Clarke after becoming an honorary letterman of Geneva. Geneva teams have had no more enthusiastic supporter nor Geneva students a more loyal friend than Boomer.

themselves with issues of fairness on college campuses. The most sensitive issue of the time was racial bias, and the federal government addressed this issue by denying tax-exempt status to colleges that would not disavow discriminatory behavior. Geneva had always accepted African-American students, back to the days of the freedmen after the Civil War. Their numbers declined in the early twentieth century, but by 1970 there was a significant African-American presence on campus, including faculty members. Geneva admitted African-American students—they lived in dormitories, participated in activities, were elected to campus offices, were an accepted part of the campus community. It was true that African-American students faced attitudes and incidents of prejudice on campus. But it was not institutionalized

Virginia Napoli was appointed director of women's athletics in 1975. This position grew in scope after Title IX, when women began an increasing schedule of intercollegiate athletics.

in rules, so that the college could in good conscience sign the statement required by the Internal Revenue Service:

In the acceptance of persons as students and in all matters having to do with the adoption and administering of rules involving the rights and privileges of students that there shall be no discrimination on the basis of race, color and national or ethnic origin.

Beyond such legal statements, Geneva continued to work seriously, though not always successfully, to challenge on campus the discrimination that persists in American culture.

In the case of gender inequality, there were two specific areas where Geneva had to change its policies in order to conform to the law: dormitory rules and women's athletics. In 1975, after conferring with the Pennsylvania Commission on Human Relations and consulting with other colleges, Geneva

Graduation took place in the Field House in 1972. More recently, at least in good weather, it has been held in Reeves Field. The 1972 *Genevan*.

made the dormitory rules for women the same as those for men. Like men, women no longer had to be in their dormitories at specified hours.

In 1974, the Department of Health, Education, and Welfare issued regulations implementing Title IX of the 1964 Civil Rights Act that prohibited discrimination based on gender in athletic programs, teams, facilities, and athletic scholarships. Clarke, in reporting on the matter to the Board of Trustees, stated:

We are . . . in substantial agreement with the basic thrust of Title IX and anticipate that we will probably be making major changes in the future. Ideally these changes will be made not only because of legal requirements, but more importantly because of our Christian concern that we increase the number and quality of opportunities for our women students for which Title IX provides some excellent guidelines.

Geneva had already begun enlarging the athletic program for women. Intercollegiate volleyball began in 1972–73; tennis and basketball were added the next year. Softball became an intercollegiate sport in 1979. Staff, budgets, choice of sports, and facilities were moving toward equality. By 1975, women's games were played in the Metheny Field House where the men played. The post of Director of Women's Athletics grew in responsibility with the increasing number of intercollegiate sports for women and Virginia Napoli was appointed to the position in 1975. Scholarships became available for women athletes and coaches began recruiting for women's teams.

At the request of the Student Senate a new calendar began in September 1972. Classes began earlier in the fall and the first semester ended before Christmas. Faculty and students welcomed this change, because it removed the awkwardly brief return to classes between vacation and examinations. The second semester ended in early May, giving students earlier access to summer jobs. For the free time during May, the college developed an innovative program

Stewart Lee talks with Elizabeth Hanford Dole during her visit to Geneva in 1978. At that time she was a member of the Federal Trade Commission. Professor Lee is an authority on consumer economics. He was chairman of the President's Consumer Advisory Council 1975–77 and has been a member of many boards and committees serving consumer interests. The 1978 *Genevan*.

called "Experimester" as an option for students. Faculty members were encouraged to experiment: what could they do with the freedom of a course that met all day every day for three weeks? Creativity blossomed. Traditional courses were taught in non-traditional ways. New courses were developed—a popular one in photography, a seminar on Beaver County history and sociology using the local community to illustrate national themes, a study of the Bible as literature, a course in spring flowers and insects, learning to sail in Long Island Sound. Students traveled: to England; to the art museums of Europe; to Greece and Asia Minor in the footsteps of Paul; to Israel; to the Southwest to study Indian anthropology; and to West Virginia to study the flora and fauna of the mountains.

The core curriculum was reviewed and largely kept. Geneva believed, as it had a century before, that there is a core of knowledge, ideas, and experience that ought to be part of a college education. Other colleges were excitedly moving back to that principle, which Geneva had always held. But of course there were small changes in the core. Two three-

It Happened in the 1970s

• The end of compulsory class attendance.

• The gift to Geneva of the Armstrong Cork Company plant at the foot of College Hill in 1969 and 1974—no more aroma of burnt cork. After reviewing possible uses for the land, Geneva decided to return it to its function of a century before, when it was known as Belvedere Park and was the site for Geneva athletic events.

• Recognition for Richard Michael, Geneva's Grounds Superintendent, from the National Professional Grounds Management Society for the best maintained school or university grounds in the country.

• The shortage of heating gas brought an unscheduled vacation for most of February 1977.

• The Beach Boys and other well-known groups came for the Big Name Show.

• In 1975 the Pennsylvania State Education Association was chosen to represent maintenance, custodial, and cafeteria workers. There were strikes in 1975 and 1979. Since then negotiations have produced contracts acceptable to both parties.

hour courses in Bible history replaced the four-semester sequence in Old and New Testament; a course entitled "Foundations of Christian Thought" was added. The political science requirement was shortened to one semester, with several social science options for the other semester. The language requirement could now be satisfied also by mathematics or computer science, seen

to be alternate means of communication. A controversial requirement of a course in creative and performing arts was added, on the grounds that students ought to have such experience as part of their education. The curriculum was changing in other ways. New degrees were offered in mechanical and electrical engineering and in computer science. Paul Arnold taught the first computer

course at Geneva and introduced the possibilities of computers to students, faculty, and administration.

In the midst of all these changes, Geneva was continuing to change at its heart. The *Foundational Concepts*, adopted in the 1960s, became more operative in college life, giving the college a clearer sense of purpose. The changes in recruitment practices for both students and faculty were affecting the religious makeup of the Geneva community. Willard McMillan and John H. White provided creative and faithful leadership. The chapel format was changed. It had been difficult to make the short periods set aside for chapel significant. In 1972, a new program was begun, providing for an hour-long chapel period each week. For three chapel periods a month students had a choice of small groups for Bible study, for prayer, or for discussion of significant topics or of meeting in a larger group for worship. Once a month the college met together for convocations in the Field House, for the student body had long outgrown the chapel in Old Main.

In 1970, Geneva received a grant from the Thomas F. Staley Foundation which supported annual lectureships to bring distinguished Christian scholars to the campus for two or three days. The annual Christian Faith and the Arts Week continued the series of poets, novelists, musicians, and artists who visited Geneva. The Geneva community had an opportunity to hear Francis Schaeffer and Os Guinness of L'Abri, John Perkins from Voice of Calvary, John Gerstner and R. C. Sproul. Senator Mark Hatfield addressed the convocation honoring Geneva's 125th birthday. At Geneva Charles Colson made his first public address after his release from prison, in gratitude for the support Professor Charles Givler and his family had given him after his conversion. For the annual Sports Convocation, Christian athletes Bob Richards and Bobby Richardson were among the speakers.

According to the *Foundational Concepts*, one purpose of Christian education is "to develop the student's capacity for the enjoyment of the world as God's creation, in all its cultural richness." Therefore, a range of visitors

from public life were invited to the campus: John Ciardi and Gwendolyn Brooks, poets; Rod MacLeish, radio commentator; U.S. Senator Richard Lugar; consumer advocates Ralph Nader, Betty Furness, and Elizabeth Hanford Dole.

Students had increased contact with intercollegiate Christian groups. In 1971, thirty-seven students went with chemistry professor Martin Price to the Urbana Missions Conference, sponsored by the InterVarsity Christian Fellowship, a reminder of Geneva's participation in the Student Volunteer Movement before World War I. Geneva began a cooperative program with Young Life, creating a Youth Ministries major with Roger Harlan at its head. John Guest's Coalition for Christian Outreach had a major influence on Geneva students, both through its annual Jubilee Conferences and through the presence of CCO staff members in many positions in the college. Students reached out beyond the campus. New Song was a college-sponsored group for summer ministry. Students organized music groups for programs in local churches; among these

John Guest, then rector of St. Stephen's Episcopal Church in Sewickley, Pennsylvania, and founder of the Coalition for Christian Outreach, has been a frequent speaker at Geneva. The evangelical Christian witness of that congregation has been a blessing to Geneva faculty and students. The 1974 *Genevan*.

groups were Reflection, Sounds of Joy, Children of Light, and New Creation. There was an annual work day to help elderly people in the community with needed repairs.

Geneva was one of the founding members of the Association of Reformed Colleges, which developed a program for faculty enrichment. Its purpose was not simply to exhort teachers to "teach Christianly," but to provide help in doing it. Its first venture, in 1974, assigned Nicholas Wolterstorff of Calvin College to write a working document, which he entitled "The Christian Faith, the Nature of Explanations, and the Educational Task," and to visit colleges for an intensive three-day discussion of it. Geneva was also a charter member of the Coalition of Christian Colleges. Begun in 1977 as a voice in Washington for institutions like Geneva, it soon broadened its activities. One of its most significant services was the American Studies Program, a remarkably conceived semester in Washington, D.C. Students studied the policy process and served as interns in a

variety of agencies. Through a series of case studies they pondered how their commitment to Jesus Christ might wisely affect public life in America. The Coalition also provided studies dealing with the teaching of academic fields from a Christian perspective.

In 1978, Geneva began its sponsorship of the Center for Urban Theological Studies, in Philadelphia. The Center was the outgrowth of the desire of William Krispin to make college courses accessible to pastors and laymen in inner-city churches. The growing enrollment meant that the program was serving its students well; soon students were able through the Center to pursue a Geneva degree.

During a period of growth in student body and facilities, of changing student attitudes, and of a deepening commitment to the service of Christ, President Clarke had led the college well. After a presidency that extended over twenty-four years, he announced his retirement to take effect in 1980.

At the 1996 Homecoming ground was broken on the south campus for a new academic building, then still unnamed. The architect's rendering suggests what the building will look like.

ELEVEN

INNOVATION IN EDUCATION

1980 — 1997

"The mission of Geneva College is to educate and minister to a diverse community of students for the purpose of developing servant-leaders, transforming society for the Kingdom of Christ."

The Board of Trustees elected one of its own members, Donald W. Felker, to succeed Clarke. Felker, a graduate of Geneva and of the Reformed Presbyterian Theological Seminary, had served as pastor of the Orlando, Florida, Reformed Presbyterian congregation. He later earned his Ph.D. degree from Indiana University, then for twelve years was head of the Department of Child Development and Family Studies at Purdue University. Felker was committed to the cause of Christian education and had a vigorous sense of the ways in which he hoped Geneva might become more effective in providing it. At his first meeting with the board, he outlined an impressive list of short-term goals. One of his stated concerns was to achieve a leaner operating budget that would allow more flexibility for initiatives to improve the academic program. But as he began to suggest specific moves he hoped to make in program and personnel, he alarmed much of the faculty. He did not articulate his goals for the college in such a way as to retain their support. After two years that were difficult for both president and

faculty, Felker resigned in 1983. The Board of Trustees, after long discussion, accepted his resignation. President Emeritus Clarke returned for a year as acting president.

The trustees elected another of their number, W. Joseph McFarland, as

President Donald W. Felker
Donald W. Felker (1932–1992) served as president of Geneva from 1980 to 1983.

Geneva's seventeenth president. McFarland had attended Geneva and was a graduate of Sterling College, with a Ph.D. from the University of Kansas. At the time of his election, he was serving as Director of Academic Affairs for the Board of Regents of the State of Kansas.

McFarland had a personal concern for the physical image of the college. His most dramatic project was the cleaning of Old Main's stone exterior. No one living could remember when the stone had not been a dark and depressing gray, clothed in the soot of decades. The cleaning surprised everyone by revealing the lightness of its original color, brightening the look of the whole campus. (McFarland left one soot-covered stone untouched, with a plaque reading: LEST WE FORGET.) Almost as dramatic were the changes in the interior. The chapel/auditorium had not functioned well since the disabling surgery on its stage decades before. In 1985 the stage was redesigned, enlarged, and rebuilt in oak, the memorably uncomfortable old chapel seats replaced, and the auditorium later air-conditioned. With its splendid acoustics, the auditorium became an

William Krispin, whose concern for African-American pastors combined with his creative imagination led to the creation of C.U.T.S.

The Center for Urban Theological Studies, Philadelphia, has been affiliated with Geneva since 1978.

attractive and much-used setting for many kinds of college activities. The need for interior reconstruction in Old Main was the occasion for remodeling the lobby with well-crafted woodwork, new lighting, and a carpet with the seal of the college. Gradually the classrooms were reclaimed from their scarred paneling and patched plaster, keeping the original spirit of the building, but providing a more pleasant atmosphere for teaching and learning.

The row of dwellings along Park Place, built about the turn of the century by people who enjoyed the prestige of a location facing the college, had been gradually acquired by Geneva and used for faculty and student housing and for offices. One by one they were now removed. Thanks to the removal also of the factory buildings from the Armstrong property, Old Main could again be seen on its imposing site as it had been a century before. Ferncliffe was remodeled in 1986. The restored conference rooms on the first floor housed McCartney memorabilia; faculty members had offices in the rest of the building.

A new building project during this period was an addition to the Metheny Field House. When the women's athletic program moved from antiquated quarters in the old Johnston Gymnasium, the Field House no longer had adequate space for both intercollegiate athletics and the extensive intramural program. The addition was dedicated in 1989 and named for W. Clair and Melba Merriman, Geneva Class of 1929, who had contributed substantially to make its completion possible. The new athletic complex adjacent to Reeves Field created from the land where the Armstrong Cork Company factory stood was also named in honor of the Merrimans.

During McFarland's presidency several innovative academic programs were added to the curriculum. In cooperation with the Community College of Beaver County, Geneva began a popular major in aviation. Training in business was combined with courses in music for a music-business major. In 1987, Geneva began its first graduate program, offering a master's degree in professional psy-

Men from the Genevans, the Eight Bells, do a bit of barbershop. The 1987 *Genevan.*

Henry "Toona" Hansard joined the staff of the Coalition for Christian Outreach on his graduation from Geneva in 1980; he returned to work with Jack White in campus ministry, particularly in developing activities for young people in the community and at Allencrest, the Juvenile Detention Center for Beaver County.

chology, to meet the increasing opportunity for people committed to serve Jesus Christ in professional counseling. The reaffirmation of Geneva's accreditation by the Middle States Association in 1988 included accreditation of this graduate program.

One of the most visible additions to the Geneva curriculum was the Degree Completion Program, begun in 1988. Like the Extension Program of the past, the DCP offered a non-traditional route to a college degree. As its name suggests, students who had finished two years of college work could take concentrated courses in the evening to complete a degree in human resource management. This was a carefully conceived program, well administered by Robert Hough, and students responded enthusiastically to it.

As was true across the country, the 1980s were a quieter time on college campuses than the 1970s. The pendulum of interest swung away from social and institutional issues. But students demonstrated other concerns. In 1981, engineering professor Marvin VanderWal took a group of students on a mission trip to Haiti, an experience that has been periodically repeated. Students have helped construct buildings for mission activities and have themselves been sensitized in the process. Twice the trips generated special excitement, when political turmoil in Haiti kept students from returning on schedule. On both occasions they were kept from serious danger. Students from Geneva participated in the programs sponsored by the Coalition of Christian Colleges in Costa Rica and in Russia. A number of education majors did their student teaching in mission schools abroad. The Youth Ministries program led students into a variety of activities with local churches and in the community.

Below: The 1986 Geneva Marching Band in a formal picture. They enliven the half-time shows at football games with their fine musicianship, and each spring they give a splendid concert. Their director, Donald Kephart, is seated at the left of the front row. The 1986 Genevan.

Like most Geneva presidents, McFarland was enthusiastic about athletics, and his administration coincided with a very successful period for Geneva sports. Both men and women did well. In 1987 the football team under Coach Eugene Sullivan had an 8-2 season, defeating Bluffton and Westminster to go to the NAIA Final Four national tournament. Beginning in 1988, the men's basketball team under Coach Jerry Slocum had winning seasons; as in the 1950s Geneva represented Pennsylvania in the NAIA basketball nationals. The cross-country team, coached by Steve Huggins, took four district championships between

President William Joseph McFarland
W. Joseph McFarland (1929–) was inaugurated president of Geneva in 1984 and served in that office until 1992.

In 1989, the Merriman Gymnasium was constructed to increase the facilities in Metheny Field House. It contains an additional basketball court, racquet ball courts, and offices for the staff of the department.

Students in Washington for the 1990 March for Life help fill Pennsylvania Avenue to protest the *Roe v. Wade* decision legalizing abortion.

1985 and 1989, regularly going to the National Christian College Athletic Association nationals. The baseball team won the district championship in 1982 and had consistently winning seasons thereafter, gaining the first national ranking in Geneva baseball history. Geneva's newest intercollegiate sport was men's soccer, begun as a club and recognized as an intercollegiate sport in 1972. Geneva was the district champion in 1982, 1984, and again in 1990.

The women's volleyball team went to the NCCAA finals in Marion, Indiana, in 1986, to the NAIA playoffs in 1988 and to the NCCAA national meet in 1990. The women's tennis team went to the NAIA national meet in 1987, 1988,

and 1992. The women's basketball team ranked third at the NCCAA finals in 1987 and were in the NAIA District 18 playoffs in 1988 and 1991. The soccer team ranked thirteenth in the nation in 1988; in 1989, it won the district tournament and went to the nationals. In 1991, Geneva women took the District 18 title in track; and individuals qualified for both NAIA and NCCAA national meets.

Geneva's success in intercollegiate sports continued into the administration

These Geneva students are on a mission trip to Haiti with Brad Frey and Roger Harlan. Photograph courtesy Bradshaw Frey.

of President White, who followed McFarland. Both in football and men's basketball, the White years were exciting, with teams going to the NAIA nationals in both sports. The 1995 football team finished the regular season 9-1, the best record since 1930. In 1995 and 1996 it qualified for the sixteen-team National Playoffs. In 1996, nine players received All-American honors. In 1996, the basketball team advanced to the NAIA quarterfinals, defeating the ninth- and eighth-seeded teams before losing to top-seeded Georgetown (Kentucky). In 1993 and 1996 the baseball team played in the NAIA World Series. The women's basketball team had a 20-win season in 1995.

Above: Charles Hawthrone. During his basketball career at Geneva he scored more points than any Pennsylvania collegiate player had done up to that time. Despite some outstanding Geneva players since then, he still holds the Geneva record for career points scored. The 1985 *Genevan*.

O Theophilus was written and produced by Jeff Barker, director of theater at Geneva, in 1984. It is a musical portraying the history of the early church as recorded in the Book of Acts. Here Paul (Doug Bradbury) is seen with Priscilla (Michele Kosboth) and Aquila (David Nehilla).

In 1991, President McFarland indicated his intention to resign, after eight years as college president. Chosen to succeed him was John H. White, who had been serving as Vice President for Spiritual Activities at Geneva since 1970. A graduate of Geneva in 1958 and of the Reformed Presbyterian Seminary, he received his doctor of ministry degree from the Pittsburgh Theological Seminary. His activities beyond the Geneva campus made him well acquainted with the Reformed and evangelical community with which Geneva identifies. He served as president of the National Association of Evangelicals from 1988 to 1990, and from 1994 to 1997 he was chairman of the board of NAE's World Relief. He has been on the board of Westminster Theological Seminary in Philadelphia since 1982.

As president, White set Geneva to the task of defining its mission, putting its aims into sharper focus. The college community shared in developing the following Mission Statement:

The mission of Geneva College is to educate and minister to a diverse community of students for the purpose of developing servant-leaders, transforming society for the Kingdom of Christ. We accomplish this through biblically-based programs and services marked by excellence and anchored by the historic, evangelical, and reformed Christian faith. The curriculum is rooted in the liberal arts and sciences, vocationally focused, and delivered through traditional and innovative programs.

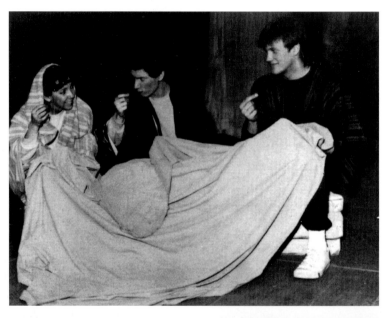

In this scene from *O Theophilus*, Peter (Dan Meharg) and John (Mark Heckathorne), with another disciple, are eavesdropping on the speech of Gamaliel before the Sanhedrin.

Freshman Orientation, 1985. Orientation activities now focus less on humiliation and more on acquainting students with each other and on making the transition into college life. The 1986 *Genevan*.

As Geneva acquired George Manor and other private houses around the campus, they were used for several purposes. George Manor was used at different times for faculty housing, student housing, and faculty offices; in the 1940s it even housed Geneva's brief experiment with a home economics department. George Manor and the other Park Place houses were razed in the 1980s.

Houses like Luger Lodge and
Northwood Hall lacked some of the
facilities of campus dormitories, but
the students who lived in them often
developed a special sense of belonging.

The college choir, the Genevans, directed by Professor Robert Copeland, tours Europe every four years. In 1994, they sang at the palace of Frederick the Great in Potsdam, where they were photographed. They also were able to sing a Bach motet in the Thomaskirche in Leipzig where Bach had been the Kantor.

In 1995, the Bagpiper presented the premier of a new musical on the life of the Biblical heroine, *Ruth*.

During the 1992–1993 season the Bagpiper Theater staged *You Can't Take It With You*. Actors on stage in this scene are Randy Bray, Chris Huggins, Sid Henriquez, Vicki Mann, and Louis Hutmire.

President McFarland leads the opening convocation procession to Metheny Field House. The 1988 *Genevan*.

David and Ann Wollman and Paul and Shirley Kilpatrick of the faculty are pictured here with Angela Ho, Annie Chen, Theresa Chou, Phyllis Fan, and Cherie Yeh from Taiwan. Geneva has had a special relationship with Christ College in Taipei through its president, Jonathan Chao, class of 1962.

Student ministry groups of many kinds are an important part of campus life. Here the Cotton Candy Connection uses puppets to share the Christian faith with youngsters. The 1992 *Genevan*.

Athletics in the 1990s

Geneva scheduled intercollegiate athletic competition in fourteen sports, seven for men and seven for women. (The track and cross-country teams consist of both men and women.) These pictures are of the 1995–1996 teams. During these years, Geneva teams participated regularly in post-season playoffs.

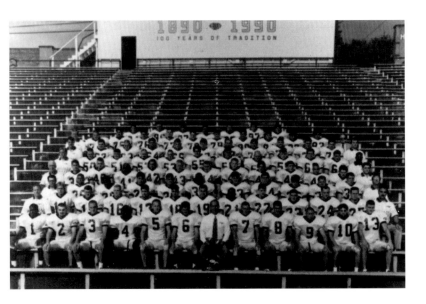

In 1993, Geneva reenacted the first collegiate basketball game in history, played by Geneva in the original Geneva gymnasium against the New Brighton YMCA April 8, 1893. The game was named basketball for a good reason.

It Happened in the the 1980s

• Annual tuition climbed past the $10,000 level.
• The Genevans under Robert Copeland took their first European tour.
• Tiger Pause opened across from the Beaver Falls Middle School and became a popular drop-in spot for after school.
• The impressive quality of the marching band under Professor Donald Kephart enhanced football games in the fall. The band's exciting spring concerts were a musical delight.
• In 1985, Geneva began a forensics competition for area high school students; now more than 350 students participate each year.

The college thus reaffirmed its quarter-century-long commitment to the *Foundational Concepts of Christian Education*, of which White had been one of the authors. The centrality of that commitment was expressed not only by the quality of the Bible courses and of the speakers in chapel and convocation services, but also in classrooms and in extracurricular activities. As part of the tenure process faculty members were required to prepare working papers exploring how their Christian faith affected their view of the subject matter of their disciplines. The college was anchored in the historic Christian faith.

But its mission also included training servant-leaders who would carry that faith into the world. Fostering diversity on its own campus was one means to that end. By its choice of trustees, its employment practices, and in the recruitment of students, Geneva worked to broaden its own community. The student body became more international. The International Students Organization has in its membership nationals from many countries, joined by "missionary kids" and other students who have grown up abroad; they help to make the campus more cosmopolitan. A special association with Christ College in Taipei, whose president was Geneva alumnus Jonathan Chao, has led to a considerable presence of Chinese students from Taiwan at Geneva. Professor Norman Carson and President McFarland celebrated their retirement from Geneva by spending time in Taipei, making those ties more personal. Geneva students visited Christ College; then traveled into mainland China to teach English at a teachers' college in Canton. Through host families Geneva created a program to welcome students from abroad and to ease the culture and language shock they confronted when they enrolled in an American college.

President John Hugh White.
John Hugh White (1936–) was inaugurated president of Geneva in 1992.

Beyond its own campus, Geneva and the Center for Urban Theological Studies (CUTS) strengthened their mutual support as the two institutions exchanged members on their boards of trustees. At commencement exercises held in Philadelphia, Geneva confers its degrees on students who complete the CUTS program.

Geneva students have continued to be servants of Christ in communicating His truth and His love in many ways: singing in musical groups; working with Habitat for Humanity and with Tiger Pause, a drop-in ministry near the Beaver Falls Middle School School; going to Europe for summer ministry with Athletes in Action. The college is

gratified that the John Templeton Foundation has included Geneva on its Honor Roll for Character Building Colleges since the award was begun in 1989.

An intriguing example of servant-leadership has been the creation of the Center for Technology Development, through which the college makes its resources of faculty, students, and laboratories available to industries lacking research facilities to develop their ideas. The program has served over sixty companies in developing and marketing products. Its director is physics professor John Pinkerton, who earlier involved Geneva students in research projects for the U.S. Bureau of Mines laboratory in Pittsburgh.

During the early years of White's presidency, two new graduate programs were begun, both with a clear purpose of preparing servant-leaders. One is the Master's Degree in Organizational Leadership, an outgrowth of the Degree Completion Program. Its purpose is to train people entering the fields of business and industry in the principles and practice of servant-leadership, recognizing the health these principles bring to the workplace. The other is a Master's Degree in Higher Education, established at the suggestion of the Coalition for Christian Outreach to provide graduate training for its staff, who now serve on forty-five campuses.

Along with these innovations, the college has continued and enhanced the excellence of existing programs. It has been able to attract highly qualified faculty members to fill positions as they open; this is particularly important because of the recent retirement of a number of respected faculty members who spent their careers at Geneva. Departments restructure their curricula, making sure their programs meet the needs of current graduates. Departments that provide professional education are maintaining or seeking accreditation from the appropriate agencies. Most recently, the Department of Engineering has been approved by the Accreditation

Provost James N. Boelkins came to Geneva from his position as chairman of the Department of Pharmacology at the University of North Dakota Medical School. He joined the Geneva faculty as vice president for academic affairs in 1985. He has been both an innovator in the development of new academic programs at Geneva and an encouraging and supportive leader for existing programs.

Gerald Moran, librarian since 1975, has presided over the McCartney Library as it moves into the information age. Students and faculty appreciate the electronic aids that make the search for information faster and easier.

John E. Pinkerton, professor of electrical engineering, joined the faculty in 1965. He is also the director of the Center for Technology Development, offering research assistance to small companies in the area.

It Happened in the 1990s

•No more registration day in the Field House; the computer now largely handles the paperwork.

•In the five years from 1992 to 1996 Geneva debate teams took three first places and two second places in the Pennsylvania College Energy Debates.

•The Museum for the Industrial Heritage of Beaver County opened on the edge of campus under the direction of history professor David Wollman. The collection centers around memorabilia from the Jones & Laughlin Steel Company, the collection of Donald Inman.

•Geneva was accredited by the Accreditation Board for Engineering and Technology (ABET).

•PennDot's long-talked-of program for relocating PA Route 18 is still being talked of.

Tiger Pause is an after school drop-in center near the Beaver Falls Middle School, where young people can build relationships with Geneva students. The center is also used for Bible studies and for tutoring programs.

A nearby McDonald's restaurant celebrated the steel tradition of the area in its design, using material from Geneva's Museum of the Industrial Heritage of Beaver County. At the center of the picture are Professor David Wollman, the director of the museum, and Donald Inman, who presented his collection to the museum. Photograph courtesy David W. Wollman.

Board for Engineering and Technology. In 1994, Geneva began an honors program for its ablest students. The C. M. Lee Distinguished Scholars, the Presidential Scholars, the Trustees' Scholars, and other students who have demonstrated unusual academic competence participate in it. About twenty students from each entering class are involved. Through honors courses and independent projects, their abilities are challenged and "iron sharpens iron." An asset for them is Geneva's proximity to Pittsburgh's cultural and educational opportunities.

Given the long concern of Geneva and the Reformed Presbyterian Church for the relationship of the Christian faith to political life, a creative venture is the establishment of the Center for Law and Public Policy, with Bradley Jacob as director. From national conferences of Christian leaders on public policy to pizza nights when Geneva students argue Christian positions on current issues, the CLPP has become a force on the campus and far beyond it.

This is an exciting time to be celebrating an anniversary of Geneva College.

Richard South came to Geneva as a chemist in 1961. He now serves as chairperson of the Department of Computer Science and Physics.

Harry Farra joined the Geneva faculty in 1966 and is now the chairperson of the Department of Speech and Visual Communication. He is a recognized authority on preaching, especially the sermons of Clarence E. Macartney, and has written books on prayer. The 1991 *Genevan*.

Philip Van Bruggen is the chairperson of the Department of Psychology and supervises the master's program in professional psychology.

Remembering

In his inaugural address in 1992, President White called the Geneva community to "Remember!"

There is much to remember in the century and a half of Geneva's history.

Each member of the Geneva family has a personal "remembering"—valued friends; faculty who helped to shape lives; times of fun, of disappointment, of growth; the excitement of learning and the hard work of study; hearing the good news of Jesus Christ and responding to it, in rejection perhaps, or in glad acceptance.

Collectively, too, the Geneva family has a "remembering." As we look back over Geneva's history, we remember:

• leaders who imagined—and turned possibilities into reality, setting their stamp on the college;

•followers who provided the resources and abilities to sustain the college;

• students who came to work—and to play;

• crises, when the college barely survived;

• times of decision, through which Geneva defined the sort of college it intended to be;

• failures, when the college was not true to its calling and did not serve its students as it should have, spiritually or academically;

• times of success and joy, when hopes were fulfilled.

But above all we remember the faithfulness and the grace of God

• Who against all the human odds has preserved the college;

• Who against the tide of the times has preserved Geneva's commitment to the Christian faith;

• Who has deepened its understanding of its biblical foundations;

• Who has caused it to grow in the number of people whom it is privileged to serve;

• Who, in spite of its failures, has kept Geneva committed to the service of Jesus Christ and His Kingdom.

All of this we remember, in order to be today, in the further words of President White "faithful to a rich and powerful heritage, and by God's grace, to make it relevant for today and tomorrow."

Homecoming still brings alumni back to the campus, as it first did in 1920.

The Homecoming Court is from 1990, when Linda Nienhuis was the queen, with her attendants and their escorts.

In 1989 New Headland House was decorated as a Swiss chalet to carry out the theme of "Geneva Around the World."

In a photograph from the 1991 parade, Tara Byler is waving from a float.

In 1959 Geneva teams became the Golden Tornadoes, suggesting the power of the storm that unroofed the chapel in 1912. (Before that, Geneva teams had been called "Covies," for "Covenanters," an honored name for Reformed Presbyterians from their origin in seventeenth-century Scotland.) Here a "tornado" appears at a 1989 football game. The 1990 *Genevan.*

Students from Geneva visited the Supreme Court on a trip sponsored by the Center for Law and Public Policy. The case: Could the University of Virginia deny funds to a student publication on the sole ground that it was overtly Christian? A highlight of their visit was a conference with Justice Ginsburg.

January 17, 1997

THE CABINET

Volume 119 **The Official Student Newspaper of Geneva College** **Number 13**

On Campus

Ahh! There's nothing like a relaxing weekend after a full week of classes! Tonight, head to Coffee Etc. for the coffee house at 10. Saturday, go to the dedication for the Habitat for Humanity house at 10 a.m. before going to watch the Lady GTs at 7 p.m. On Monday, sleep in until 9:30 a.m. -- when the MLK Day celebration starts. Go to the convo, musical, and concert, and get credit for all three. What a deal!

Weather

National Weather Service
01:00 -- 01/17/97
Friday: Partly sunny. Windy. High in the teens.
Saturday: Partly cloudy. Flurries. High 15-20.
Sunday: Mostly cloudy. Breezy and cold with high of 15-20.

Fun and games?
Building parking plans monopolize lot

David Packard
Staff Reporter

Take the little dog around the board, and if you can buy Boardwalk and Park Place then things usually work out for the best.

Such is the case in Monopoly, but things are rarely that simple in the real world, as aptly displayed by the delay in constructing the new academic building.

This new addition was slated to start full construction on this coming Monday, but something unusual occurred which centers on our own Park Place.

Park Place (or the Commuter Lot) was found to be property of Beaver Falls.

Sound surprising?

It certainly surprised both college and city officials since it is the main entrance to Geneva.

Due to this unexpected turn of events, Geneva must acquire a permit from the city to move Park Place 30 feet south.

Right now Geneva is hoping they can start construction while simultaneously moving toward the permit.

If they can do both at once, then construction may start within a week, but if the city decides they need the permit first then the earth moving equipment will wait for approximately five weeks.

James MacDonald, vice president for Business and Finance, explained it best stating the two scenarios as either the "process (to obtain the permit) before construction or the process during construction" with the latter being preferred.

This problem will hopefully be resolved in the next several days, but once construction begins the campus community will have some problems of its own.

The main problems: where will the commuters park, and where will the new entrance be once Park Place is closed?

Since both problems have been expected by Physical

> "Spring Alley [the road in front of Metheny Fieldhouse] will temporarily become the college's main entrance while Park Place is moved."
>
> -- Rick Smith, Dir. of Physical Plant

Plant and Student Development, answers have been sought.

Rick Smith, director of physical plant, said that "Spring Alley (the road in front of Metheny Fieldhouse) will temporarily become the college's main entrance while Park Place is moved."

This road, which currently serves as a one-way exit, will now become a one-way entrance while the main (and only) exit will be over by Pearce Hall.

Since parking problems were also foreseen, Dean of Students Joy Jewell, had the Director of Security, Bob Jones, conduct a survey comparing the number of parking spaces lost to those available in other lots.

During construction, all the spaces from Route 18 to Science and Engineering building will be lost, but the parking behind S&E will remain. Those spaces were counted and totaled 49 spaces still available for parking.

The proposed solution to overcome the loss of spaces was the lot behind New Headland which is also known as the Freshman Lot.

During the time of this survey, it was noted that on average there were 51 spaces open in this lot, so commuters are encouraged to park there while Park Place is moved.

One other lot that could be better utilized is the one behind Metheny Fieldhouse, since it usually has open spaces as well.

Obviously, this will prove a slight nuisance to commuters, but fortunately, provisions have been made to deal with the situation, and if all remain patient, things will return to normal by the end of this calender year.

Smith believes these plans "to be the least disruptive to the campus" and will be implemented upon the start of construction, (either in five days or five weeks) so expect to see these new traffic patterns in the next few weeks.

Photo courtesy Public Relations

Parking may be tight now due to construction, but look at what the future holds.

The front page of *The Cabinet*, the student newspaper, for January 17, 1997, comments about the changed traffic patterns caused by the construction of a classroom building. *The Cabinet* has been published for 118 years.

GENEVA COLLEGE
1848 ━━━━━ 1998
PRO CHRISTO ET PATRIA

On the Occasion of Geneva's Sesquicentennial

We Honor The Presidents of Geneva College . . .   . . . And We Salute Their Wives

John Black Johnston, 1848 – 1850	*Elizabeth Boyd Johnston*
William Finney George, 1850 – 1852	*Martha Speer George*
James Renwick Willson Sloane, 1852 – 1856	*Margaret Milligan Sloane*
John Calvin Knox Milligan, 1856 – 1858	*Rachel Farrington Milligan*
John Calvin Smith, 1858 – 1860	*Sarah McCartney Smith*
Nathan Robinson Johnston, 1865 – 1867	*Rosamond Rogers Johnston*
Samuel John Crowe, 1867 – 1871	*Amanda Geddes Crowe*
Henry Hosick George, 1872 – 1890	*Sarah Brown George*
William Pollock Johnston, 1890 – 1907	*Clara Anderson Johnston*
William Henry George, 1907 – 1916	
Renwick Harper Martin, 1916 – 1920	*Alice Garrett Martin*
Archibald Anderson Johnston, 1920 – 1923	*Marion Love Johnston*
McLeod Milligan Pearce, 1923 – 1948	*Carrie McKaig Pearce*
Charles Marston Lee, 1948 – 1956	*Alice Stewart Lee*
Edwin Cameron Clarke, 1956 – 1980	*Agnes Thorburn Clarke*
Donald William Felker, 1980 – 1983	*Evelyn Harrington Felker*
Edwin Cameron Clarke, 1983 – 1984	*Agnes Thorburn Clarke*
William Joseph McFarland, 1984 – 1992	*Roberta Dill McFarland*
John Hugh White, 1992–	*Norma Woods White*

Sources

Secondary Sources

In 1908, for the sixtieth anniversary of Geneva, W. M. Glasgow wrote a history of the college, *The Geneva Book*. His lifelong association with the college, his research, the documents he reproduced, and his biographies of its graduates make the work an invaluable source for the early history.

On the occasion of the college centennial in 1948, J. Vale Downie began a history, which was published serially in the *Geneva Alumnus*. It is a lighthearted account, including many of his own memories and those of his family.

The research of Robert M. Copeland for his "The Presidents of Geneva" (an unpublished manuscript) has been of great value.

Primary Sources

The Board of Trustees graciously allowed me access to the minutes of the board, complete since 1880. Reports of the Board of Trustees to the annual meetings of the Synod of the Reformed Presbyterian Church and articles in church periodicals have also been useful. Other primary sources include the catalogs of the college; files of *The Cabinet*, the college magazine and newspaper, reaching back to its beginning in 1879; the *Geneva Alumnus;* and copies of the *Genevan*, the college yearbook, from its beginning in 1919. McCartney Library has preserved memorabilia of many kinds that help bring the history to life.

I have also consulted courthouse documents in Logan County, Ohio, and in Beaver County, Pennsylvania. Local newspapers in both locations have been of assistance.

Index

Vice President for Spiritual
Activities, 146

Vietnam, 130

volleyball, women's, 134, 145

Vos, J. G., 96, *98*

W

Walker, Berdella, 40

Walkinshaw, J. L., *35*

Weir, Lola, *46*

Weir, Wilbur, *46*

West, Walter, 99

Westminster Theological
Seminary, 146

WGEV, *118*

White, John H., 115, *125,* 136,
146, 157, *158*

Willet, Henry Lee, 78

Willson, James Renwick, 4

Wilson, Beulah, 68

Wilson, Lumley, *127*

Witherspoon, Tillie, *30*

Wollman, Ann, *153*

Wollman, David, *153,* 160, *161*

Wolterstorff, Nicholas, 137

World Relief, 146

World War I, 61, 65

Wylie, Ava Allen, *89*

Wylie, H. H., 39, 45, 61, *63,* 67,

Wylie, H. H., Mrs., 68, 69, 84, 96

Wylie, J. H., *22*

Wylie, J. R., *27*

Wylie, Mattie, *17*

Y

YMCA, 34, 47, 49, 65, 80, *81*

Young Hall, 111

Young Life, 136

Young, Robert M., 69, 111

Youth Ministries, 142

YWCA, 34, 47, 65, 80, *81*

About the Author

David M. Carson

David M. Carson is the Samuel A. Sterrett Professor of Political Thought, Emeritus, at Geneva College. He was a member of the faculty there from 1951 until his retirement in 1992. He is a graduate of Yale University, where he was elected to Phi Beta Kappa, and of the Reformed Presbyterian Theological Seminary. He received the Ph.D. degree in History from the University of Pennsylvania in 1964. He has also published *Transplanted to America*, a history of the Reformed Presbyterian Church. He is the grandson of James M. Coleman, Sterrett Professor of Political Thought at Geneva from 1892 to 1907.

He is married to Margaret Weir, and they have two daughters, Elizabeth Wilson and Christina Townsend. Among his avocations is serving as piano accompanist for student recitals in Geneva's Department of Music.

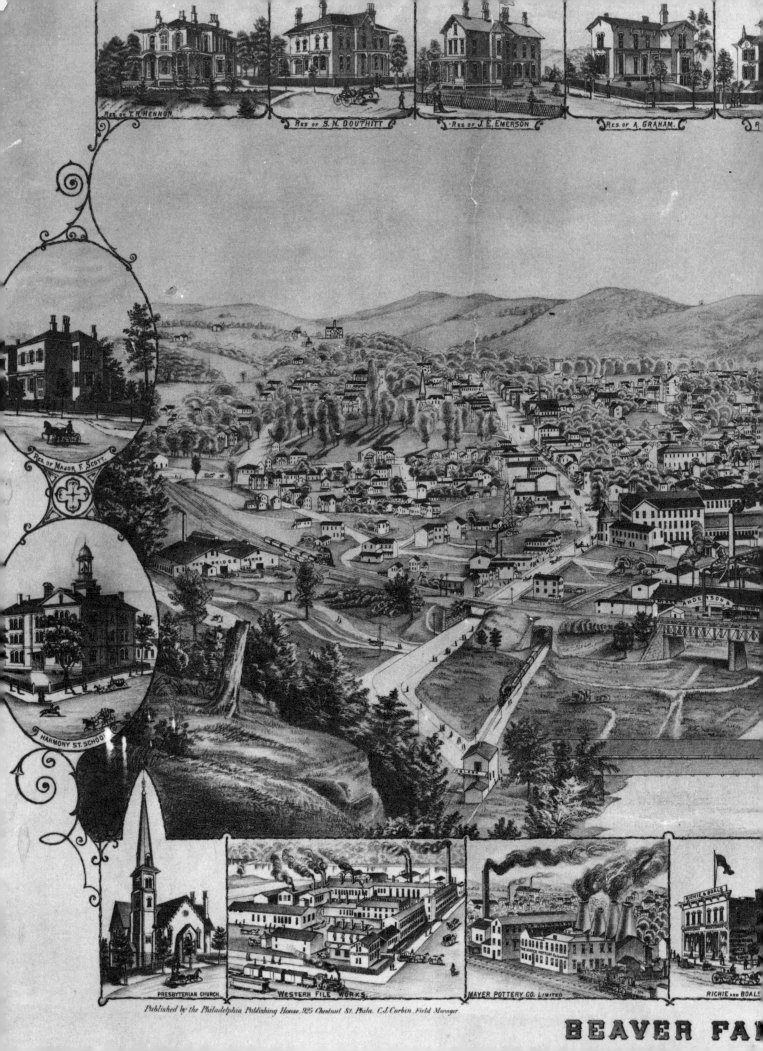

Res. of T.R. HENNON.　Res. of S.N. DOUTHITT.　Res. of J.E. EMERSON.　Res. of A. GRAHAM.

Res. of MAJOR F. SCOTT.

HARMONY ST. SCHOOL.

PRESBYTERIAN CHURCH.　WESTERN FILE WORKS.　MAYER POTTERY CO. LIMITED.　RICHIE AND BOALS

Published by the Philadelphia Publishing House, 925 Chestnut St. Phila. C.J. Corbin, Field Manager.

BEAVER FA